# Science Plus 2

General Editor Jenny Jones

Published by Collins Educational
An imprint of HarperCollins*Publishers*
77–85 Fulham Palace Road,
London W6 8JB

© HarperCollinsPublishers Ltd 1997

First published 1997

Reprinted 1997, 1998, 1999

ISBN 000 322470 8

All rights reserved. No part of this publication may be reproduced, stored in a retrieval system, or transmitted in any form or by any means, electronic, mechanical, photocopying, recording or otherwise, without the prior permission of the publisher.

The Science Plus writing team
Elizabeth Forth
Jenny Jones
Bob McDuell
Shirley Parsons
Gareth Price
Pamela Singh
Linda Welds

Designed by Chi Leung

Edited by Dodi Beardshaw

Picture research by Caroline Thompson

Artwork by Barking Dog Art, Russell Birkett, Tom Cross, Jerry Fowler

Printed and bound in Singapore

## Acknowledgements

Every effort has been made to contact the holders of copyright material, but if any have been inadvertently overlooked, the publishers will be pleased to make the necessary arrangements at the first opportunity.

**Photographs**
The publishers would like to thank the following for permission to reproduce photographs:
(T = top, B = bottom, C = centre, L = left, R = right)
Allsport 72L; Allsport/C Bronskill 31, J Gichigi 59, D Rogers 72C; John Birdsall Photography 13, 16R, 26, 36R, 46, 47, 56, 66, 69R, 70; Dr E Pott/Bruce Coleman Ltd 21; The Old Bushmills Distillery Co Ltd 45L; City of Newcastle upon Tyne 50; Derby Evening Telegraph 49C; Ecoscene/A Jones 38, C Gryniewicz 55; Eye Ubiquitous/J Dakers 22; Ford Motor Co Ltd 74; A Radford/Fortean Picture Library 43C; Geophotos 33B, 61; Ronald Grant Archive 68; Andrew Phillips/IHPVA 75; P Steele/ICCE 9; Warner Brothers (courtesy Kobal) 27, 58; 20th Century Fox (courtesy Kobal) 39; Andrew Lambert 60; Magic Eye (c) 1994 by N E Thing Enterprises, Inc. Reprinted with permission of Andrews & McMeel. All rights reserved. 15C; Mirror Syndication International 5, 7R, 62; NHPA/B Hawkes 48, D Woodfall 49T, A.N.T. 52; David Noble Photography 25; PC Review/Terrance Beddis 15T; 'PA' News 8; Gareth Price 67R; Rex Features Ltd 17, 33C, 34T, 71, 72R; Gavin Rowe 36L; Science Photo Library 7C, 11, 20, 23C, 32C, 44, 51, 54, 65, 67L; SHOUT Pictures 4, 6, 14, 16L, 32T, 37, 45R, 63; Ian Pillinger/Skyscan 73; Still Pictures/A Compost 10R, 19, N Cobbins 10L, A Beignet 23R, J Maier 42, L Murray 64, Mark Edwards 69L; Tony Stone Images 12, 18, 28, 29, 30, 35, 40, 41, 53; Sygma 34C; Stewart Thompson 57; THE X-FILES (c) 1996 Twentieth Century Fox Television. All rights reserved. 43T; Zefa Pictures 24, 33T.
Cover Photograph: Tony Stone Images

This book contains references to fictitious characters in fictitious case studies. For educational purposes only, the photographs have been used to accompany these case studies. The juxtaposition of photographs is not intended to identify the individual in the photograph with the character in the case study. The publishers cannot accept any responsibility for any consequences resulting from this use of photographs and case studies, except as expressly provided by law.

# Contents

**19 Gasping for breath**
19.1 A vital gas  4
19.2 Strong lungs  5
19.3 Fighting for breath  6
19.4 I don't believe it!  7

**20 Environmentally friendly**
20.1 Green spaces  8
20.2 Food chains  9
20.3 Neglecting the environment  10
20.4 Environmentally friendly  11

**21 Fooling your senses**
21.1 Going for a ride  12
21.2 Eating at the fair  13
21.3 Come on in – the water is lovely!  14
21.4 Optical illusions  15

K1 What a show!  16
K2 Growing seedlings  17

**22 Green and growing**
22.1 What can we get from plants?  18
22.2 Making a meal of plants  19
22.3 Somewhere to call home  20
22.4 Growing seeds  21

**23 Food and drink**
23.1 Algae  22
23.2 Fungi  23
23.3 Yeast  24
23.4 Bacteria  25

K3 Selling yoghurt  26
K4 Rust bucket?  27

**24 Strong stuff**
24.1 On your bike!  28
24.2 Joining up  29
24.3 Filling a gap!  30
24.4 It's a racket!  31

**25 Trapped underground**
25.1 Sediments  32
25.2 Minerals and crystals  33
25.3 Earthquake!  34
25.4 Volcanoes  35

K5 Antiques roadshow?  36
K6 Keeping fit  37

**26 How fast? How slow?**
26.1 Reactions  38
26.2 Alien blood!  39
26.3 Setting hard  40
26.4 Enzymes  41

**27 Sorting out**
27.1 Getting the gold  42
27.2 The truth is out there  43
27.3 Cleaning the blood  44
27.4 Separating liquids  45

K7 Survival bags  46
K8 Keep it cool!  47

**28 Our school's rubbish**
28.1 Is it all rubbish?  48
28.2 What a gas!  49
28.3 Burning rubbish  50
28.4 Different fuels  51

**29 Who needs energy?**
29.1 Sources and uses  52
29.2 Non-renewable energy sources  53
29.3 Renewable energy sources  54
29.4 Waste not, want not  55

K9 Cooking times  56
K10 Dog's dinner  57

**30 In the balance**
30.1 Chain gang  58
30.2 Big Frank  59
30.3 Well balanced  60
30.4 Bridges  61

**31 Music machines**
31.1 The concert  62
31.2 The recording studio  63
31.3 Whale song  64
31.4 Ears  65

K11 Hospital garden  66
K12 Recycle it!  67

**32 Hot stuff**
32.1 Special effects  68
32.2 Cooking  69
32.3 Keeping food warm  70
32.4 Using energy  71

**33 Movement**
33.1 Pushes and pulls  72
33.2 Up, up and away  73
33.3 Stopping forces  74
33.4 Keeping going  75

**Glossary**  76

# 19 Gasping for breath

## 19.1 A vital gas

These firefighters have a dangerous job. If they do not have **oxygen** to breathe they will die.

- Can you think of other people who need to carry oxygen with them?
- Where does the oxygen that you breathe usually come from?

Every cell in your body needs **energy**. The **glucose** from food reacts with the oxygen to provide energy. This process is called **respiration**.

Glucose + oxygen → energy + carbon dioxide + water

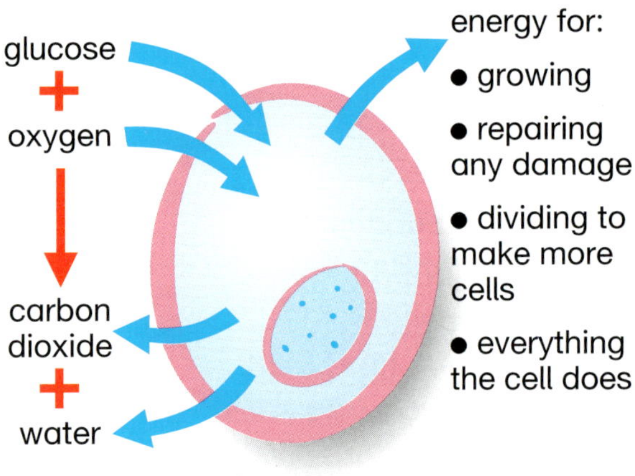

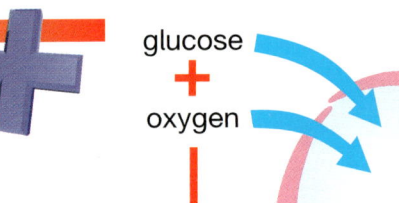

The water and carbon dioxide are waste products. You get rid of them when you breathe out. On a cold day you can see the moisture in your breath. You cannot see the **carbon dioxide** because it is a colourless gas.

glucose + oxygen → carbon dioxide + water

energy for:
- growing
- repairing any damage
- dividing to make more cells
- everything the cell does

1. Why do firefighters carry oxygen in the fire engines?
2. Where does the glucose in the cells of the body come from?
3. What is made when glucose reacts with oxygen?
4. Explain why you cannot see carbon dioxide.

**Key words**

**oxygen
energy
glucose
respiration
carbon dioxide**

## 19.2 Strong lungs

This man has a strong pair of lungs! Not! It is the muscles around the ribs that control how hard he can blow.

- Can you feel your ribs moving when you breathe?
- Do they move further if you breathe more deeply?

The volume of air that people can hold in their lungs varies. An average man can hold 5–6 litres of air in his lungs. A fit athlete may hold 7 litres. A small child has a smaller lung capacity.

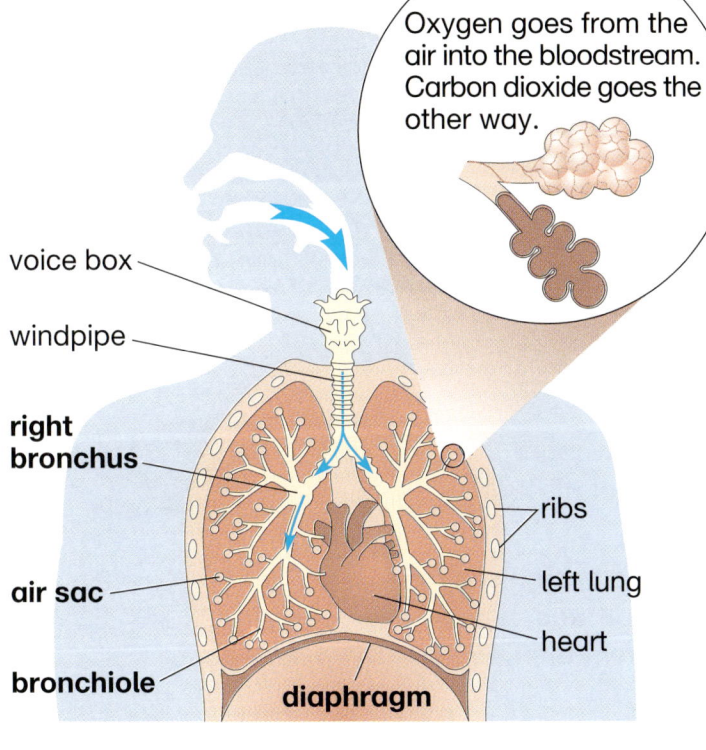

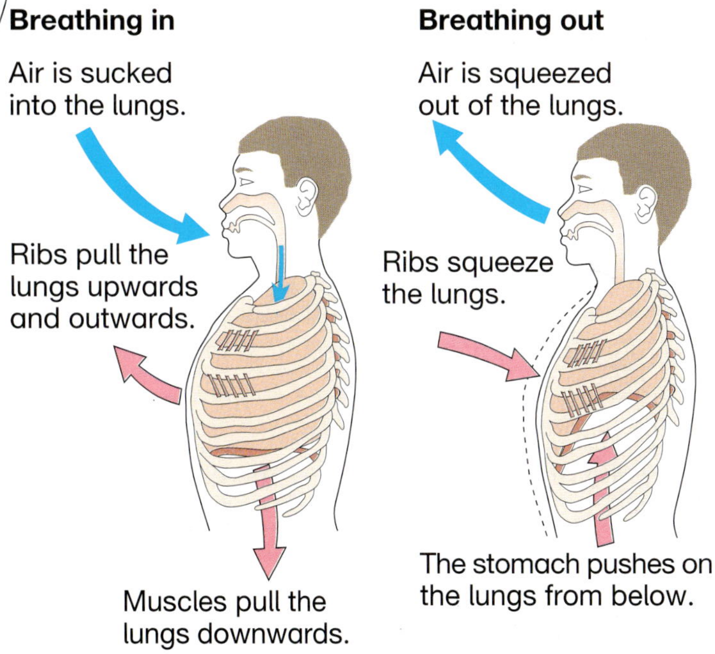

Oxygen goes from the air into the bloodstream. Carbon dioxide goes the other way.

voice box
windpipe
**right bronchus**
**air sac**
**bronchiole**
ribs
left lung
heart
diaphragm

**Breathing in**
Air is sucked into the lungs.
Ribs pull the lungs upwards and outwards.
Muscles pull the lungs downwards.

**Breathing out**
Air is squeezed out of the lungs.
Ribs squeeze the lungs.
The stomach pushes on the lungs from below.

1. Which direction do the ribs move when someone breathes in?
2. What is the name of the tube that carries air from your mouth to your lungs?
3. What happens to the air when it reaches the air sacs?
4. Draw a flow chart to show how air gets from the mouth to the air sacs.

**Key words**

**bronchus**
**bronchiole**
**air sac**
**diaphragm**

5

## 19.3 Fighting for breath

This girl has **asthma**. Asthma is a condition that causes the **airways** to narrow. This stops a person breathing out properly. The **symptoms** that people with asthma have are coughing, wheezing and being short of breath.

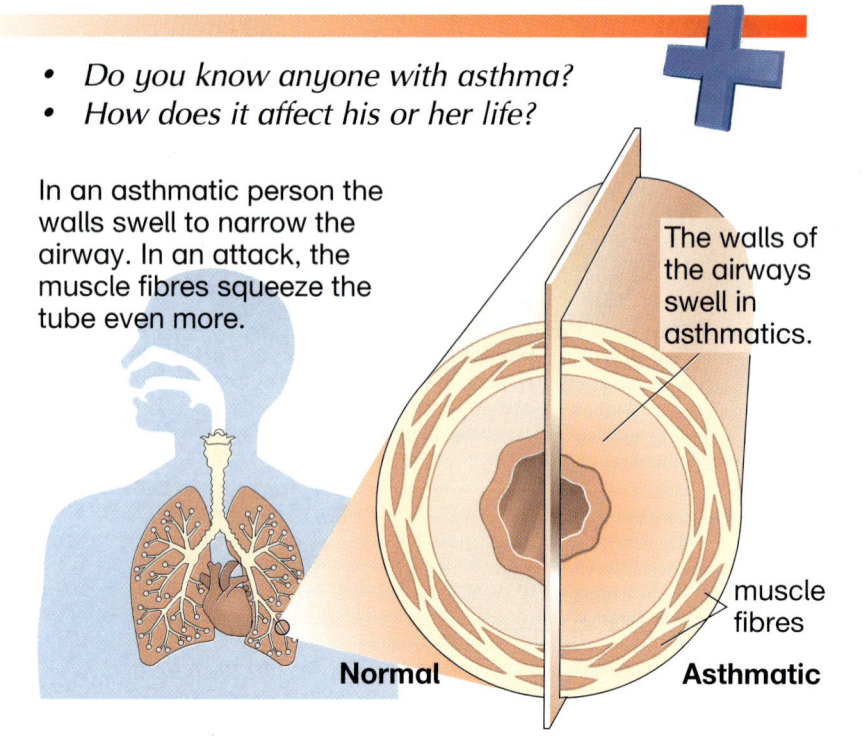

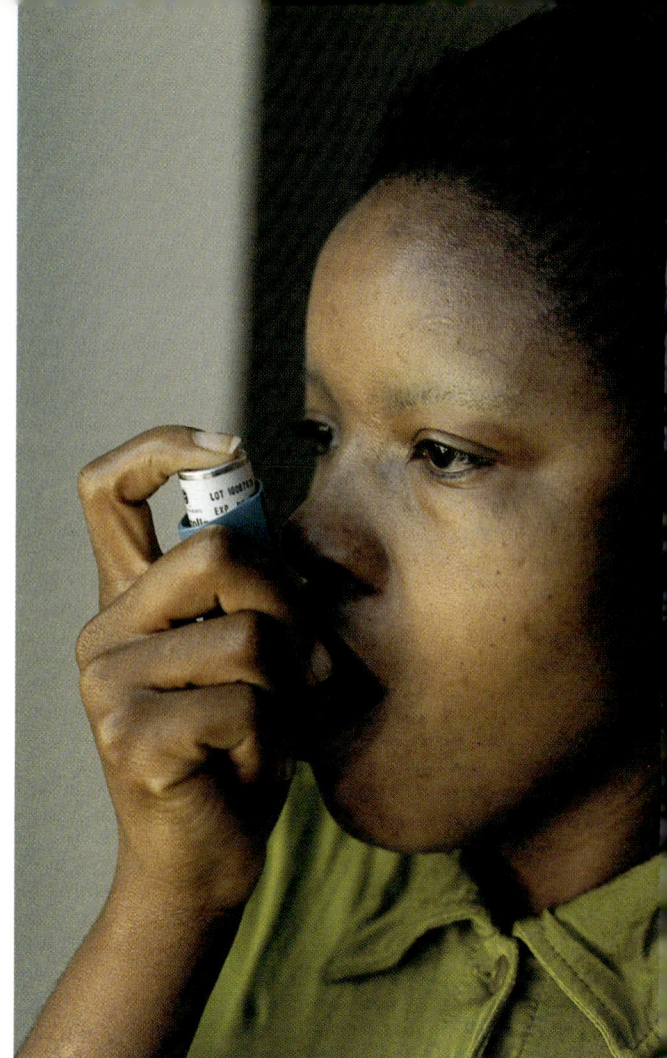

- *Do you know anyone with asthma?*
- *How does it affect his or her life?*

In an asthmatic person the walls swell to narrow the airway. In an attack, the muscle fibres squeeze the tube even more.

The walls of the airways swell in asthmatics.

muscle fibres

**Normal**   **Asthmatic**

Asthma reduces:
– the speed that people can breathe in and out
– the total volume of air the lungs can hold.
This is because the walls of the airways swell. The airways will get narrower after exercise or if the air is polluted. The amount of air that the lungs can hold will be reduced in asthma sufferers.

People with asthma may need to use an **inhaler** like the one being used in the picture above. There are two types of inhaler. The doctor may also prescribe other drugs that are **protectors**. They help to prevent another attack.

| Type of inhaler | Effect |
| --- | --- |
| Reliever | Relieves the symptoms. Makes breathing easier. |
| Protector | Helps to keep the airways open. Patient feels better. |

1. Describe what happens to the airways of people with asthma.
2. Why do people with asthma need inhalers?
3. Design a poster for the wall of a sports centre which explains the symptoms of asthma.

**Key words**

asthma
airways
symptoms
inhaler
protector

6

## 19.4 I don't believe it!

They smell. They cost a fortune and they make you ill. But people still buy cigarettes – I don't believe it!

- *Why do you think people smoke? Do you smoke?*
- *Do you think that smoking should be allowed in public places?*
- *Should smoking be banned altogether?*

The arrow in this x-ray is pointing to cancer in the lungs. Scientists have proved that certain chemicals in **tobacco** smoke cause cancer. This is why there is a warning on every cigarette packet about the dangers of smoking.

☠ **Tar** – this clogs the lungs and makes colds, **bronchitis** and lung disease much more likely.

☠ Carbon monoxide – a poisonous gas which stops red blood cells carrying oxygen.

☠ **Nicotine** – an **addictive** drug that raises the heart rate.

☠ Hydrogen cyanide – a poisonous gas, used to execute condemned prisoners in the USA.

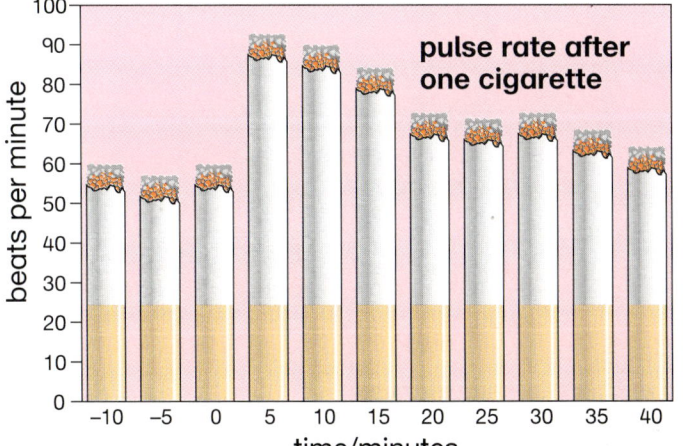

pulse rate after one cigarette

Although people who smoke know that it is harmful, they cannot stop. This means that they put their lives at risk. People who do not smoke may be 'passive' smokers if they live with other people who smoke. Passive smoking is harmful too.

1. Design a poster warning people of the dangers of smoking.
2. Your friend has asked you to help him stop smoking. How would you do this?

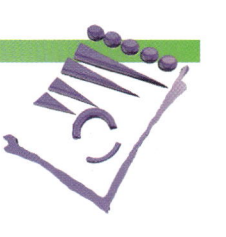

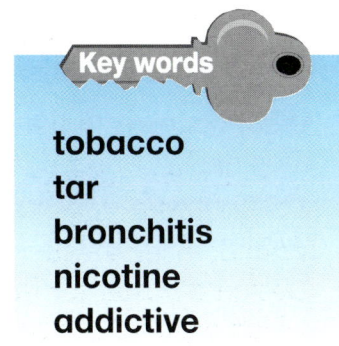

**Key words**

**tobacco**
**tar**
**bronchitis**
**nicotine**
**addictive**

# 20 Environmentally friendly

## 20.1 Green spaces

This 'green street' lasted a few days. The grass was not able to grow without soil underneath it.

- Would you like your street made into a lawn? Why?
- What green spaces do you have locally?

## The carbon cycle

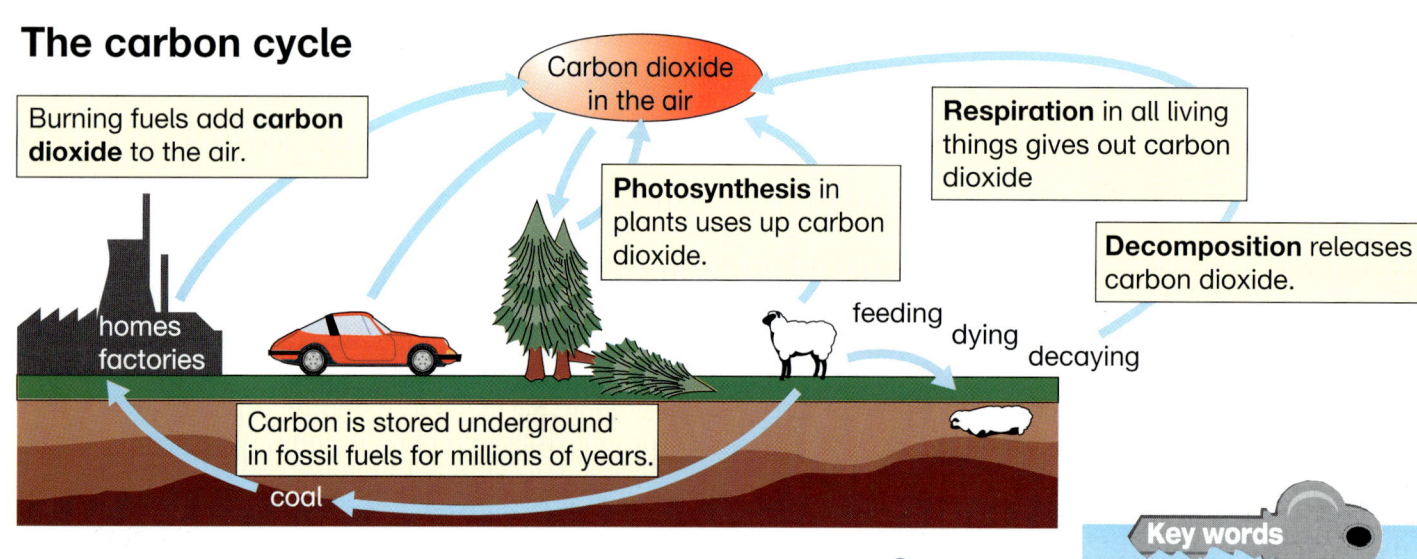

**Carbon dioxide in the air**

Burning fuels add **carbon dioxide** to the air.

**Photosynthesis** in plants uses up carbon dioxide.

**Respiration** in all living things gives out carbon dioxide

**Decomposition** releases carbon dioxide.

feeding
dying
decaying

Carbon is stored underground in fossil fuels for millions of years.

homes factories
coal

1. What happens to the carbon in living things when they die?
2. When wood is burnt what happens to the carbon dioxide given off?
3. What gas does respiration make?
4. Why do plants need carbon dioxide?
5. Give two reasons why plants are so important to animals.

**Key words**

carbon
cycle
carbon dioxide
decompose
photosynthesis
respiration

## 20.2 Food chains

- *Have you got a pond near where you live?*
- *What lives in the pond?*
- *Is it **polluted** in any way?*

The green plants are the food makers, the **producers**.
An animal that eats producers is called a **herbivore**.
Animals that eat herbivores are called **carnivores**.

A network of **food chains** that links together is called a **food web**.

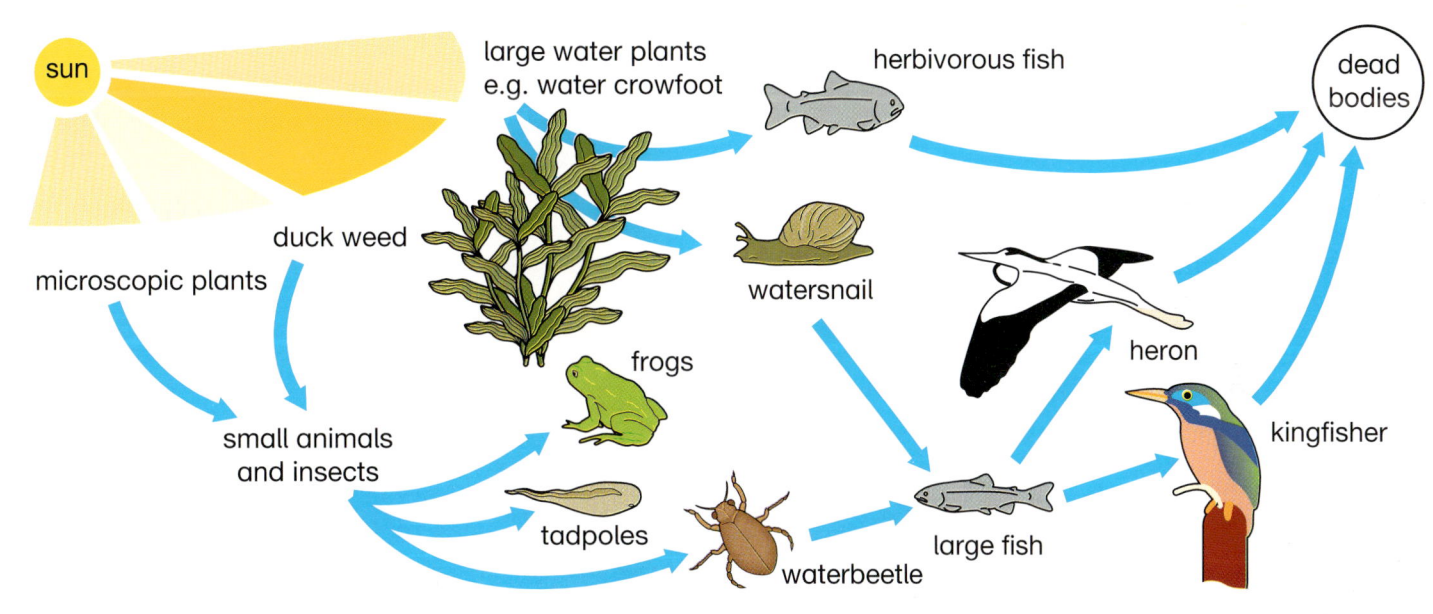

Water is polluted by rubbish, sewage and discharges from local industries. If farmers use too much fertilizer on their fields it may run off into local streams and ponds. The plants would grow too well and 'choke' the pond.

1. Write down one food chain from the pond.
2. What is a producer? Put a box around the producer in your food chain.
3. What is a herbivore? Put a line under the herbivore in your food chain.
4. What is a carnivore? Put a star by the carnivore in your food chain.

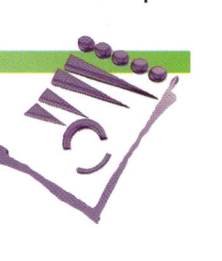

**Key words**

**pollution
producer
herbivore
carnivore
food chain
food web**

## 20.3 Neglecting the environment

Rainforests and coral reefs provide **environments** where many different types of plants and animals live. Food chains exist here too but the organisms involved often seem very strange.

- Have you ever seen any television programmes about rainforests or coral reefs?
- Why do you think that rainforests and coral reefs are so important?

Sadly many of these wonderful places are being destroyed. People fell trees for timber or to make clearings to farm the land. Coral reefs are destroyed by pollution and by divers collecting the coral to sell it. Environmental groups like Friends of the Earth and Greenpeace are working hard to slow down the rate of destruction. Laws have been made that **protect** plants and animals.

1. List some of the ways in which people damage their environment.
2. Sort your list from Question 1 into two groups: 'very damaging' and 'slightly damaging'.
3. Find out about local or national environmental pressure groups and prepare a talk to give to your group.
4. Design a poster explaining to people ways that they could help to protect the environment.

Key words

**environment**
**protect**

## 20.4 Environmentally friendly

Nowadays many shops stock products that claim to be environmentally friendly or 'green'. The **packaging** can be **recycled**. This means that it can be used again. Milk bottles are collected, cleaned and **reused**. Other glass bottles may be taken to local bottle banks. Paper may be recycled. Toilet rolls may be made from recycled paper.

- What products claim to be environmentally friendly?
- Green products are often more expensive than ordinary ones. Are they worth this extra money? Why?

Moving goods around takes up energy and can add to pollution. It may be more environmentally friendly to buy locally produced goods.

Many things we buy are over-packaged. We throw away lots of packaging. Some shops try to reduce this. Some shops encourage customers to reuse their old carrier bags.

The bottles in this pile can be recycled to make new plastic packaging.

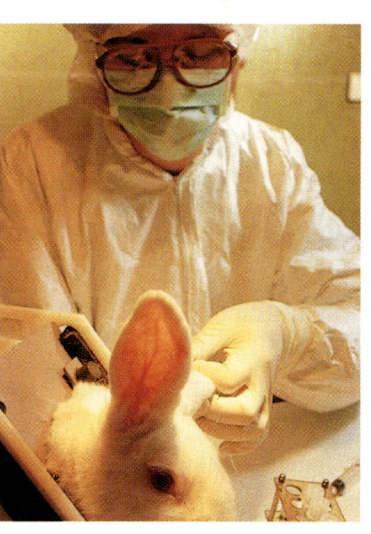

Some products have the label 'This product has not been tested on animals.'

1. List things that make a product green.
2. List things that do not make a product green.
3. What sorts of things can be recycled?
4. What can people do to be more environmentally friendly?
5. Why are people concerned about testing things on animals?

**Key words**

packaging
recycle
reused

# 21 Fooling your senses

## 21.1 Going for a ride

Alton Towers has some of the best rides in the country. You can be shaken around until you feel really sick. And people pay money for this!

- Have you ever been to a fair? What rides did you go on?
- How did you feel during the ride and when you got off?

Your ears contain **balance** organs. They tell your brain which way up you are and how you are moving.

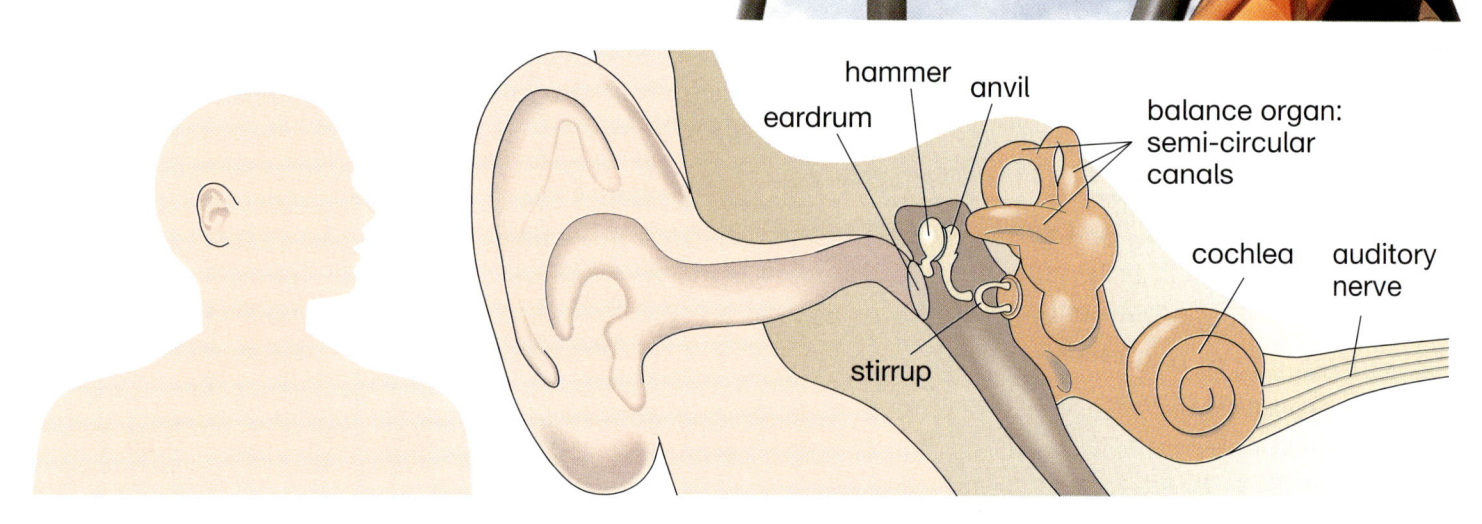

Each balance organ is made up of three small tubes which are filled with liquid and are at right angles to each other. When you move, the liquid in the tubes moves (like a spirit level). This **stimulates sensory nerves** which send impulses to your brain. When you spin, the liquid picks up speed and continues to move even when you stop. Your brain interprets this as the ground moving and you feel giddy. Skaters avoid getting giddy by keeping their eyes fixed on one point then flicking their head round.

1. Where are the balance organs in your body?
2. What are your balance organs filled with?
3. Does having your eyes open when you spin around affect how easily you become dizzy? Plan an investigation to find out.

**Key words**

balance
stimulate
sensory nerve

## 21.2 Eating at the fair

The smell is almost as good as the taste. People who sell snacks at fairs know that the smell of frying onions will often attract people to buy hot dogs and burgers.

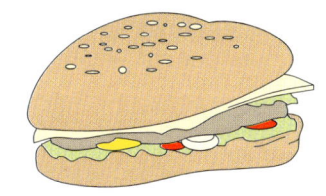

- Have you ever waited in a queue for food?
- What made you wait?
- Have you ever had a blocked nose? What did your food taste like?

Your nose is lined with millions of smell sensitive nerves. As you breathe in, chemicals in the air dissolve in the moisture in your nose. The dissolved chemicals stimulate the nerves in your nose which send information to your brain. Your nose is sensitive to millions of different smells.

Your tongue has taste sensitive nerves, called **taste buds**. You can only **detect** four tastes: sweet, sour, salt and bitter. So when you 'taste' delicious food, most of the flavour comes from the smell of the food. The taste buds for each taste are grouped in different parts of the tongue.

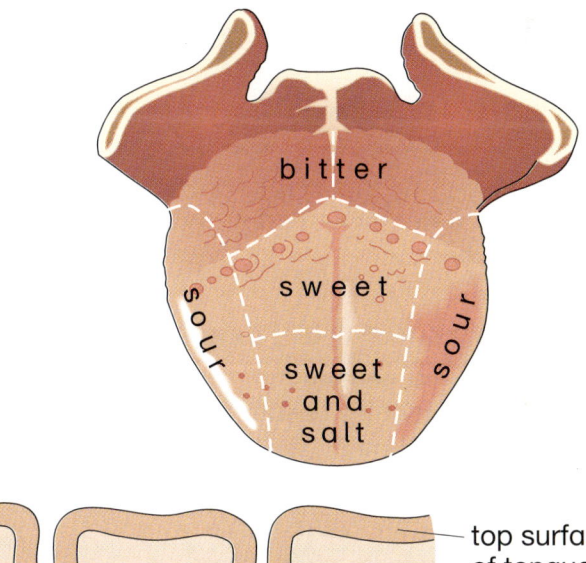

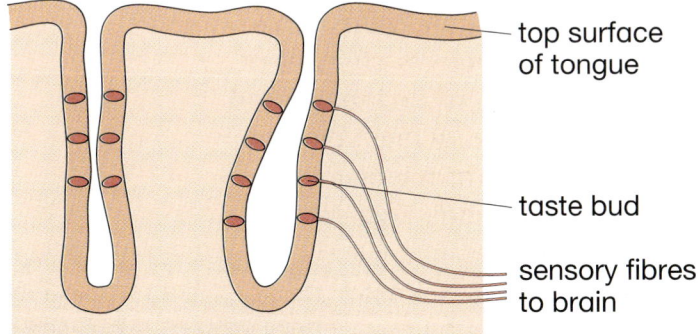

1. What are taste buds?
2. Where are taste buds found?
3. List the four tastes that your taste buds can detect.
4. Explain why food does not taste the same when you have a cold.

**Key words**

**taste buds**
**detect**

## 21.3 Come on in – the water is lovely!

Every Christmas Day people go down for a dip in the sea in Dublin. It must be freezing but they do it every year.

- Have you ever been in the sea? Was the water cold?
- How cold did the water feel after a while?

Skin contains nerves that detect **touch**, **pressure**, **pain** and **temperature**. A strong **sensation** is usually because more nerves are stimulated. Some parts of your skin are more sensitive than others because there are more nerve endings. Your skin detects *changes* of temperature. After a while it gets used to the new temperature and you feel normal again. So, warm water can feel cool if you are very hot. Your senses are fooled!

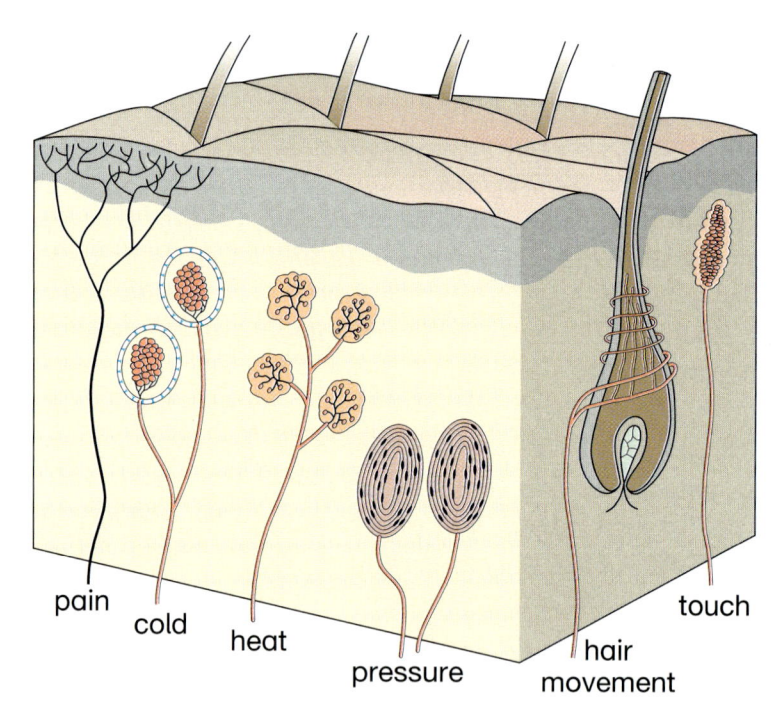

1. Draw and label a diagram of the skin.
2. Name the four stimuli that nerves in the skin can detect.
3. Why do you think pressure **sensors** are deeper in the skin than touch and pain sensors?
4. Why does a nurse test a baby's bath water with her elbow?

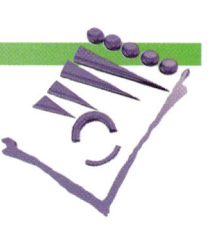

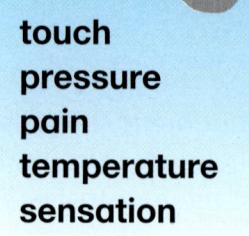

**Key words**

**touch**
**pressure**
**pain**
**temperature**
**sensation**
**sensors**

## 21.4 Optical illusions

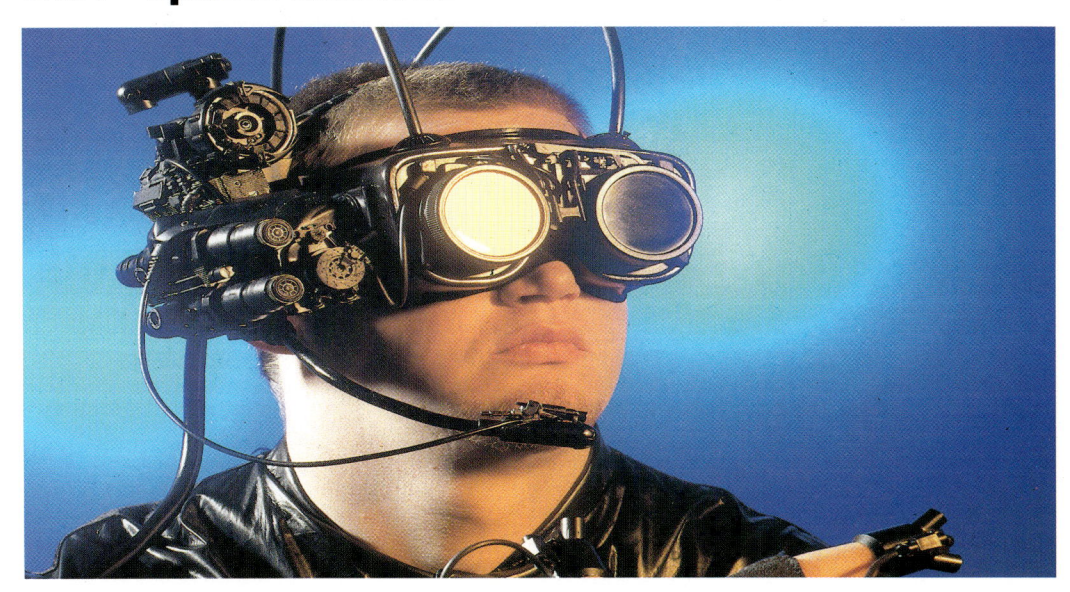

In the future we may be able to see into three-dimensional (**3-D**) virtual worlds – places that do not exist ouside a powerful computer. Already we have goggles – soon we will have whole bodysuits.

- *Would you like to explore a virtual world? Why?*
- *What else could you use these goggles for?*

Each of the eyepieces shows a slightly different view. The brain combines this information so we see in 3-D. The Victorians used photographs taken from slightly different positions to achieve this **illusion**. 3-D or **stereoscopic** vision helps us to judge distance.

Look at the pattern here and try to **focus** just behind it. You should be able to see a 3D image. This is an example of an illusion.

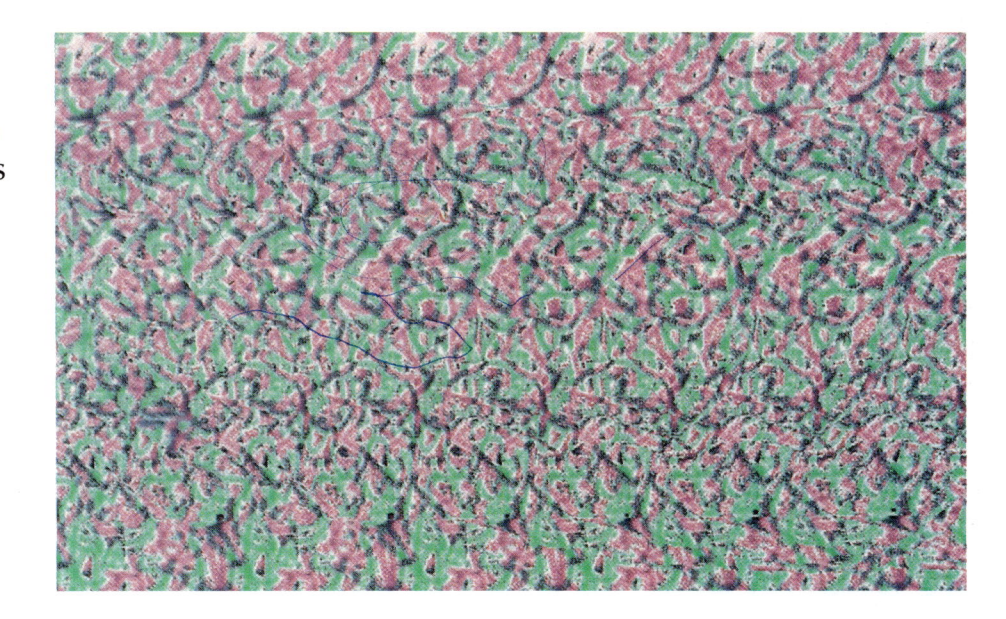

1. What 3-D image did you see?
2. Was it easy to see?
3. How did you feel when you were looking at the picture?
4. Can you see the 3-D image when you have one eye shut?

**Key words**

3-D
illusion
stereoscopic
focus

## K1  What a show!

> We get roughly 2000 visitors every week during the summer. They come to see the gardens which have some of the best flower displays in the country. I have to produce a constant supply of fresh flowers from May through to September.

- *What could happen to spoil the gardener's plans?*
- *Suggest some things she could do to make sure these problems do not spoil her display.*

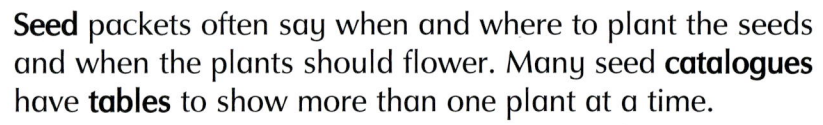

**Seed** packets often say when and where to plant the seeds and when the plants should flower. Many seed **catalogues** have **tables** to show more than one plant at a time.

|  | J | F | M | A | M | J | J | A | S | O | N | D |
|---|---|---|---|---|---|---|---|---|---|---|---|---|
| African marigold |  |  | (S) | (S) | S |  |  | F |  |  |  |  |
| Cornflower |  |  |  | (S) | S |  |  | F |  |  |  |  |
| Lupin |  |  | S |  |  | F | F |  |  |  |  |  |
| Poppy |  |  | S | S |  | F | F |  |  |  |  |  |
| Primrose |  |  |  | F |  | (S) | (S) |  | P |  |  |  |

S = Sew into ground
(S) = Sew in green house
F = Flowering
P = Plant seedling into ground for next year's flowers

1. Which seeds could the gardener plant in February?
2. Which flower is in bloom earliest in the year?
3. The busiest month of the year for tourists is August. Which flowers would you suggest the gardener plants to make sure she gets a good show in August?
4. Which flower would you recommend to give a good show in July?

**Key words**

seed
catalogue
table

## K2 Growing seedlings

*I can buy mung beans at 57p for a 250 g pack – that's over a thousand seeds. Bean sprouts are much more expensive – £1.20 for 250 g, and that's only about 70 seedlings! I want to find the cheapest way to grow mung bean seedlings to use in my salad recipes.*

- What things could affect the way the seeds grow?
- Which of these things do you think is most important? Why?

| The seed takes in water and swells. **Chemical changes** in the seed break down stored food supplies. | → | Food supplies help the **root** and **shoot** start to grow. | → | The root grows downwards towards the soil and water. The shoot grows upwards towards the light. | → | The first **leaves** develop and start to make food. |

1. Plan an investigation to find out the best way to grow mung beans for salads. Once your teacher has checked your plan, carry it out.
2. Use a word processor to write up your investigation.
3. Prepare an illustrated instruction sheet to show people the best way to germinate mung beans for salads.

**Key words**
chemical changes
root
shoot
leaves

# 22 Green and growing

## 22.1 What can we get from plants?

Plants are very useful to us. We eat them, sit on them, use them to dye our clothes and take them as medicines.

- What things have you got at home which originally came from a plant?
- What things in the classroom originally came from a plant?

Some plant materials do not have to be changed very much before we can use them. Wood only needs to be cut and preserved. Dyes can be collected by **grinding** up the plant. Other materials have to be **extracted** from the plant. **Crushing** seeds removes most of the oil but the rest can be taken out **chemically**. Medicines are removed chemically too. Perfumes are collected by **distillation**.

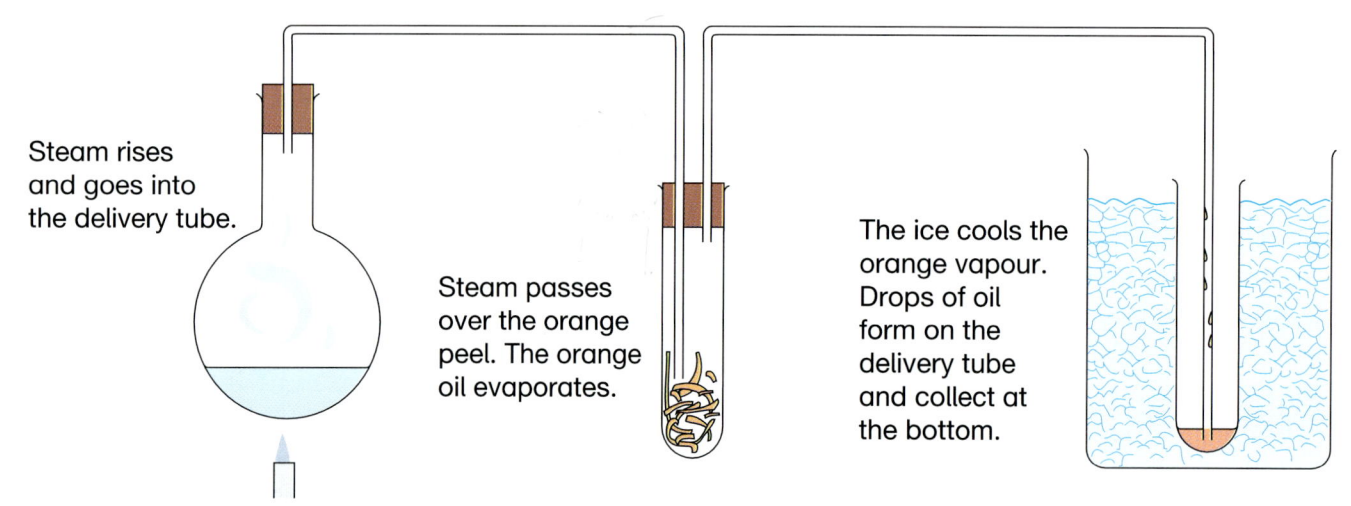

Steam rises and goes into the delivery tube.

Steam passes over the orange peel. The orange oil evaporates.

The ice cools the orange vapour. Drops of oil form on the delivery tube and collect at the bottom.

1. Name as many useful plant products as you can.
2. Sort the list into clothing, for homes, cosmetics and toiletries, and medicine.
3. Describe how orange oil can be extracted for perfumes. What name is given to this process?
4. Which seeds are used to make oil?
5. Suggest a simple way to collect the perfume from rose petals.

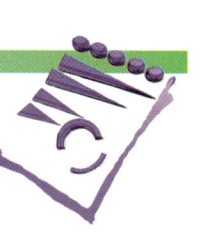

Key words

**grind**
**extract**
**crush**
**chemicals**
**distillation**

18

## 22.2 Making a meal of plants

Plants provide animals with nutrients such as carbohydrates, fats, proteins, vitamins and minerals. Some plants just add flavour. There is very little food value in many spices – but a curry without the spice would taste awful!

- List the plants you eat.
- Which plants do we usually eat raw?
- Which plants do we usually cook before eating?

**fruits and seeds**: peas, cherries
**bud**: brussel sprouts
**leaf**: spinach, lettuce
**flower**
**stem**: celery
**roots**: carrots, potato

1. Use the drawing above to list all the parts of a plant.
2. Write down a few words to explain what each part does.
3. Plan an investigation to find out if the size of an onion affects its taste.

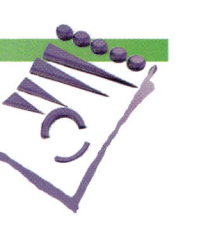

**Key words**
bud
seed
fruit
flower
stem
leaf
root

19

## 22.3 Somewhere to call home

Seedlings which grow too close to the parent plant have to compete for light, water, space and nutrients. Seeds should spread out and find a new place to survive.

Another word for spreading seeds is **dispersal**. Some plants disperse their own seeds. Some plants get help from animals, the wind or water.

- When are most seeds dispersed?
- Have you ever prepared the **soil** and planted seeds?

People plant seeds where they want them to grow. The soil is often carefully prepared to give the seeds the best chance to germinate. The type of soil affects the type of plant that will grow in it. The only plants that can grow in the dry sandy soils in **deserts** are cacti. **Waterlogged** soils in **swampy** places will have more water plants growing there. Soils with a lot of clay in them will often become waterlogged. Gardeners like good **loam** soils for growing vegetables and flowers.

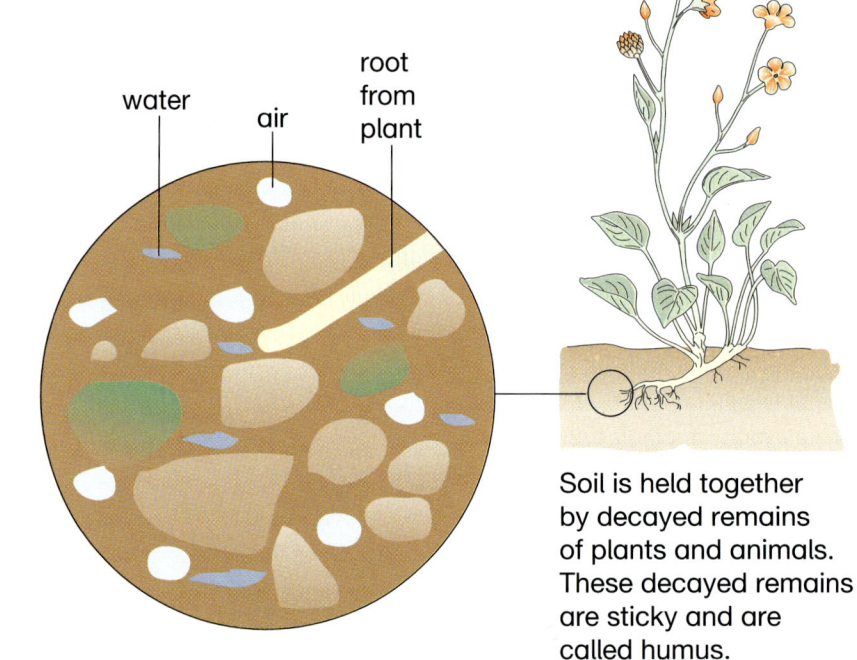

Soil is held together by decayed remains of plants and animals. These decayed remains are sticky and are called humus.

1. Draw diagrams with notes to show how some seeds may be dispersed.
2. What is soil made from?
3. What sorts of plants can grow in dry desert soils?
4. How does the type of soil affect the type of plant that grows there?

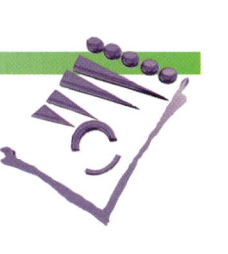

**Key words**

disperse
soil
desert
waterlog
swamp
loam

## 22.4 Growing seeds

It's amazing that this huge tree has **grown** from such a small seed. The growing conditions must have been perfect.

- What seeds do you eat?
- Why don't seeds such as rice and lentils grow when they are kept in a cupboard?
- Why can't we grow plants like bananas and oranges in this country?

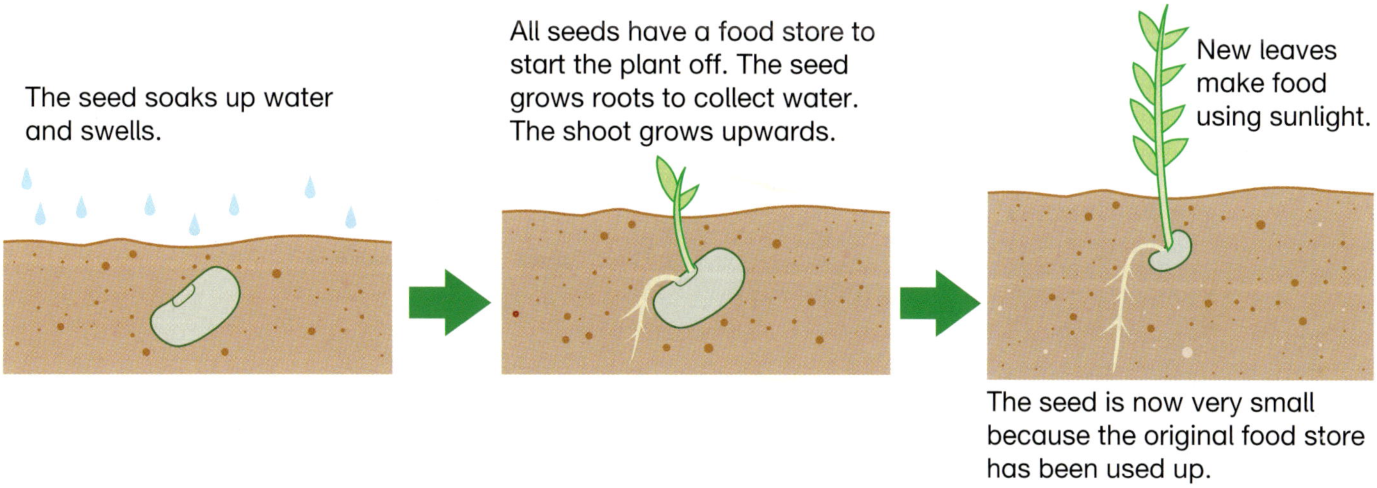

The seed soaks up water and swells.

All seeds have a food store to start the plant off. The seed grows roots to collect water. The shoot grows upwards.

New leaves make food using sunlight.

The seed is now very small because the original food store has been used up.

Seeds only grow into new plants if the conditions are right. They need water, air and warmth. Seeds do not do anything until they get what they need. The seed stays **dormant**. All seeds have a food store to start the plant off. The seed grows **roots** to collect water and new **leaves** to make more food. This early growth is called **germination**.

1. Why do plants make seeds?
2. What do seeds need to help them germinate?
3. What does germinate mean?
4. Which part of the seed grows first?
5. What is it used for?
6. Which part of the seed grows next?
7. What is it used for?

**Key words**

grow
dormant
root
leaf
germinate

21

# 23 Food and drink

## 23.1 Algae

This woman is drying **seaweed** in the sun. When it is dry and crispy it will be used in cooking. Seaweed belongs to a group of living plants called **algae**. They grow in seas and rivers all around the world. Algae are useful as a food because they contain large amounts of minerals.

- *Have you ever tasted seaweed?*
- *What do you think it tastes like?*

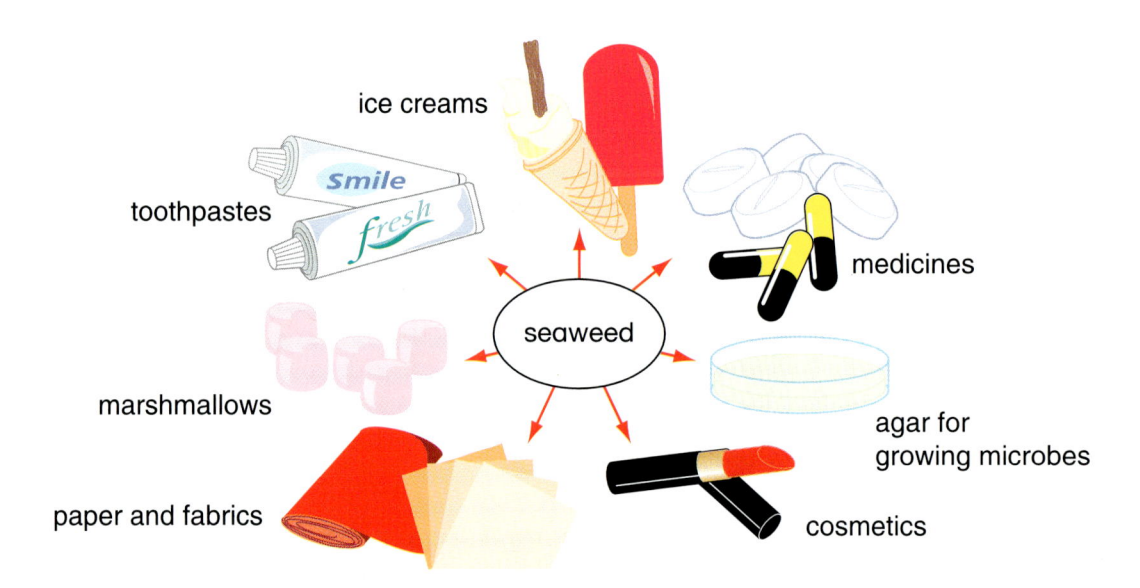

Single-celled algae are **microscopic** plants that live in water. They make ponds and fish tanks look green. Algae make **glucose** and produce **oxygen** in the light. A lot of the oxygen that we breathe on earth is made by algae in the oceans.

Carbon dioxide + water + light energy → glucose + oxygen

1. Why is seaweed a useful food?
2. What is **agar** jelly used for?
3. Why is it useful that algae produce oxygen?
4. Write out an equation to show how a green plant produces oxygen.

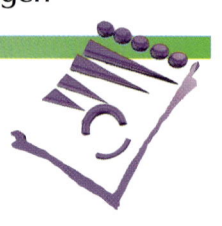

**Key words**

seaweed
algae
microscopic
glucose
oxygen
agar

## 23.2 Fungi

**Fungi** are a group of living things that cannot make their own food. They live on food that has been produced by something else. The mushrooms you buy in the supermarket probably grew on manure! Fungi are used to make **antibiotics** such as **penicillin**. Blue cheeses such as Stilton and Danish Blue have very tiny fungi added to them to give them flavour. In Japan fungi are used to make Sake wine from rice.

- *Have you ever tasted blue cheese?*
- *Do you think fungi are useful?*

This food is mouldy. It has been invaded by **microscopic** fungi. **Mould** is another name for microscopic fungi. Mould will live anywhere that it can get food and moisture and is warm enough. Microscopic fungi are too small to be seen on their own but when they multiply into thousands we can see them.

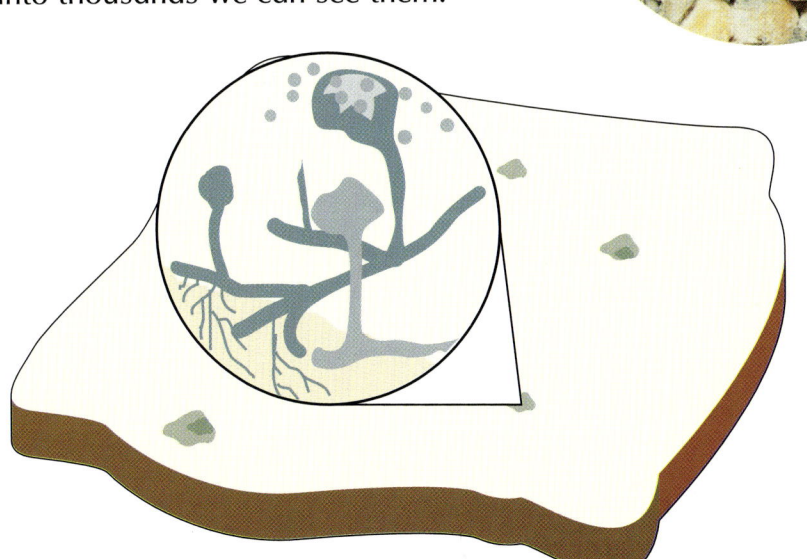

Spore lands on food in a warm, moist place.

▽

Spore grows to produce a mat of fungal threads over the food.

▽

After a while the threads produce their own spores to spread to new places.

▽

Spores travel in the air to new food sources.

1. What does the word microscopic mean?
2. What three things do fungi need to survive?
3. Make two columns. At the top of one column write the heading 'How fungi can be helpful'. At the top of the other column write the heading 'How fungi can be harmful'. Put some examples in each column.

**Key words**

**fungi**
**antibiotic**
**penicillin**
**microscopic**
**mould**

## 23.3 Yeast

These people are crushing grapes with their feet. They are going to make wine. The skin of the fruit is covered in tiny fungi called **yeasts**. They will feed on the **sugar** in the fruit and change it to **alcohol**. This is called **fermentation**.

- Have you ever seen someone making wine or beer at home?
- What are the advantages of home-brewed beer and wine?

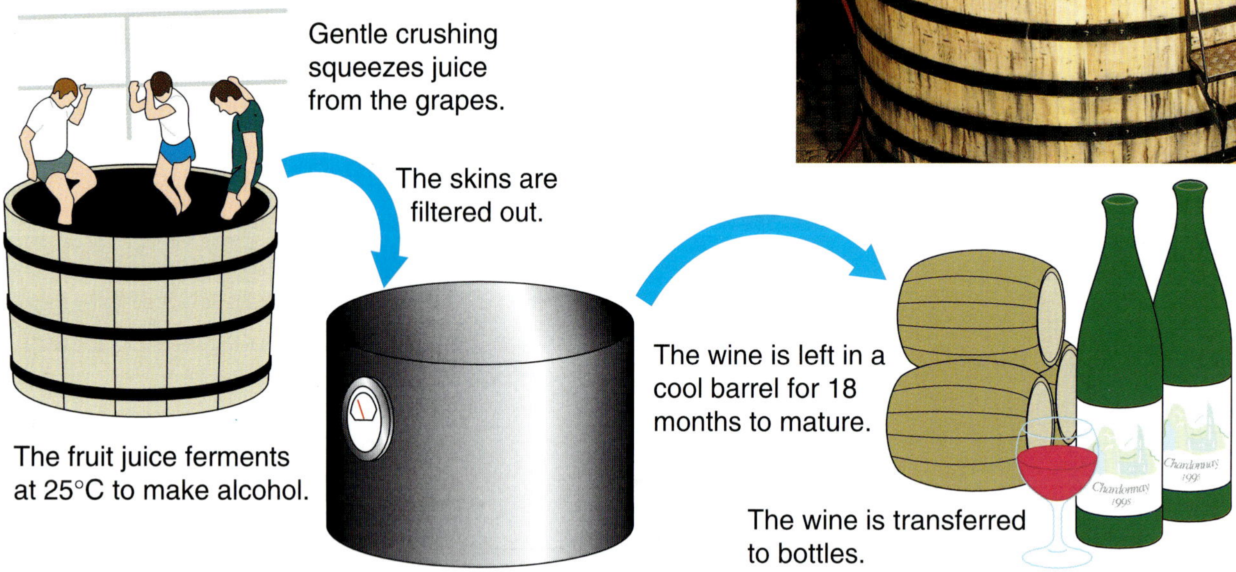

Gentle crushing squeezes juice from the grapes.

The skins are filtered out.

The fruit juice ferments at 25°C to make alcohol.

The wine is left in a cool barrel for 18 months to mature.

The wine is transferred to bottles.

Any fruit or vegetable can be used to make wine. Beer is made from barley or wheat instead of fruit. Hops are added to give the beer a bitter flavour. Yeast is made as a by-product of **brewing**. This is rich in vitamins and is used in savoury spreads. Yeasts ferment sugars to produce alcohol and **carbon dioxide**. It is the carbon dioxide that puts the bubbles into the beer, wine or champagne.

Glucose → alcohol + carbon dioxide

Fermentation is also used to make antibiotics and in baking. When the yeast in bread dough is warm and moist and has sugar to feed on, it ferments. The carbon dioxide produced makes the dough rise. The bubbles trapped in the dough make the bread light. The alcohol evaporates when the dough is cooked.

1. What two things does yeast make when it ferments sugar?
2. What conditions does yeast need to ferment?
3. Why are savoury spreads made from yeast good for you?
4. Draw a flow chart to show the stages in making wine.

**Key words**

yeast
sugar
alcohol
ferment
brew
carbon dioxide

## 23.4 Bacteria

The cheese on this Dutch market stall is called Gouda. It has a yellow waxy coating to stop it drying out and to protect it. **Bacteria** in milk make it go sour. This is the first step in the cheese-making process. Cheese may be made with milk from cows, goats or sheep.

- Have you ever eaten goat's milk cheese?
- What use do you think the **rind** could have?

Heat the milk to 73°C and then let it cool to 29°C.

↓

Now add bacteria and an **enzyme** called rennet.

↓

Rennet separates the milk into curds and a watery liquid called whey.

↓

Drain off the whey. Cut the curds into smaller lumps and add salt. → Put the curd mixture into cheese moulds and squeeze out more of the moisture. → In two days the cheeses are taken out of the moulds and left to ripen for up to two years.

Bacteria need moisture, warmth and a food supply before they can grow. Different sorts of bacteria produce different sorts of cheese. If **lactic acid bacteria** are added to milk which is then kept warm, they turn it into **yoghurt**.

1. Why is the enzyme rennet added to the milk in the cheese-making process?
2. What is added to cheese before it is put into the moulds?
3. Name the three things that bacteria need to grow.
4. Plan an investigation to find out how the temperature affects how quickly milk turns sour.

**Key words**

bacteria
rind
enzyme
lactic acid bacteria
yoghurt

# K3 Selling yoghurt

My name is Jane Lee. I am the head scientist at Dairy Foods Inc. I have to find better, cheaper ways to produce foods which we can sell to shops. One of our most popular lines is **yoghurt**. I want to know if I can use low fat milk to make yoghurt and sell it to slimmers. Would the yoghurt mixture **thicken** enough without the fat?

- What could you add to yoghurt to make it thicker?
- What sorts of yoghurts can you buy at your local shop?

| Heat the milk to **boiling** point. | → | Pour into a clean container. Cover with a teatowel and let the milk cool. | → | When it reaches 37°C stir in some natural yoghurt. | → | Keep the milk warm for a day or two. The mixture will thicken as it sets. |

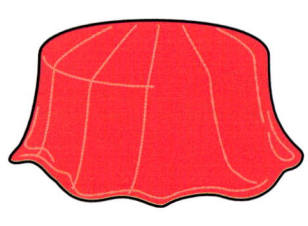

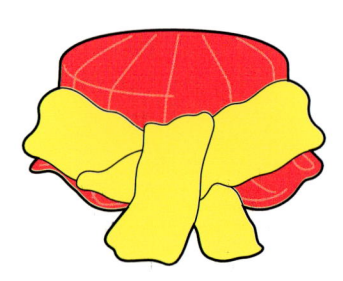

1. Plan an investigation to find out which sort of milk makes the best yoghurt. When your teacher has checked your plan, carry it out.
2. Use a word processor to write up your experiment. Include all your results.
3. Write a letter to Jane Lee to answer her question.
4. Prepare an illustrated instruction sheet to show people how to make yoghurt.

**Key words**

yoghurt
thicken
boiling

## K4  Rust bucket?

The Mad Max films are set in a future where petrol is very rare. The vehicles look a bit rusty too!

- *Where do cars usually rust?*
- *Why do you think they rust around there?*

**Rusting** is a **chemical reaction** that depends on water and air. Car manufacturers try to prevent rusting with protective layers. This keeps the air and water away from the metal underneath.

| Protective coating | Rust seen after 1 year | Rust seen after 5 years |
|---|---|---|
| Paint | No | Yes |
| Metal plating and paint | No | A little |
| Grease | No | Yes |
| Wax coating | No | No |

1. Which coating gives the best protection against rusting?
2. Survey the cars in the school car park to see which ones have the most rust.
3. Use a computer database to store the information from your survey.
4. Explain how your database would be useful to the car buyer above.

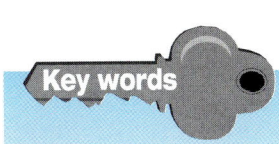

**Key words**

rust
chemical reaction
protective

# 24 Strong stuff

## 24.1 On your bike!

Mountain bikes can cost a fortune – anything from £99 to over £4000! The most expensive bikes have **alloy** frames, specially shaped handlebars and ultra-light wheels. But are they worth it?

- Have you got a mountain bike? Where do you ride it?
- How is it different from a racing bike?

| Metal or alloy | Density / g per cm$^3$ | Strength (1 = weakest) | Does it rust? |
|---|---|---|---|
| Pure iron | 7.9 | 4 | yes |
| Pure **aluminium** | 2.7 | 1 | no |
| Aluminium alloy | 2.8 | 8 | no |
| Steel alloy | 7.8 | 6 | yes |
| **Chromaloy** | 7.9 | 9 | no |

1. Which of the materials has the lowest density?
2. Which of the materials is strongest?
3. Aluminium alloy bike frames use much thicker tubing than chromaloy ones. Why?
4. Steel frames have to be painted but aluminium alloy frames do not. Why?

**Key words**

alloy
density
aluminium
chromaloy

## 24.2 Joining up

Joints that need to be strong are welded. So a mountain bike needs **welded** joints. An electrician often uses **solder** to join metal wires to a circuit board. **Alloys** are mixtures of two or more metals. The properties of an alloy may be very different to the properties of the pure metals it contains. Solder is an alloy of **tin** and **lead** that melts at a low temperature. Soldered joints are not as strong as welded ones.

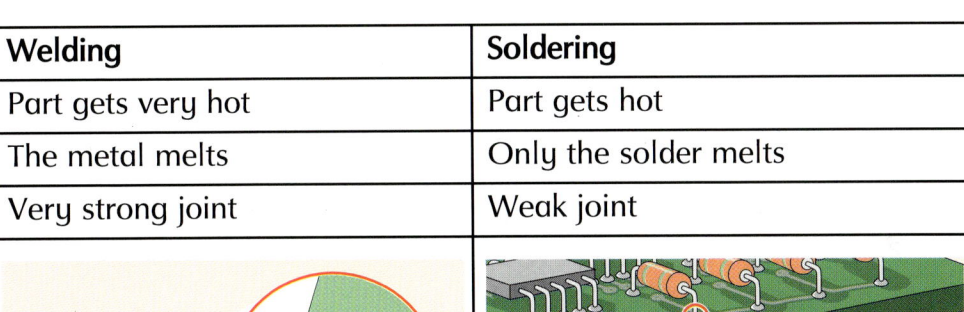

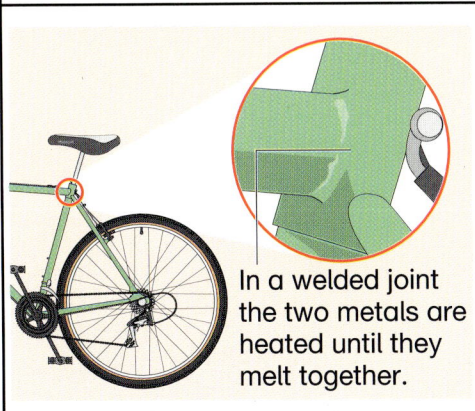

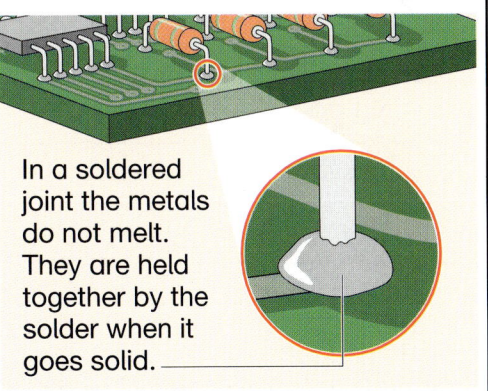

- Why is solder not used for mountain bike frames?
- Why do you think welding is not used for circuit boards?

| Welding | Soldering |
| --- | --- |
| Part gets very hot | Part gets hot |
| The metal melts | Only the solder melts |
| Very strong joint | Weak joint |

In a welded joint the two metals are heated until they melt together.

In a soldered joint the metals do not melt. They are held together by the solder when it goes solid.

1. What name is given to a mixture of metals?
2. Name the two metals solder contains.
3. Why must a welder need to take care when welding a car petrol tank?
4. Why are joints on electrical circuit boards soldered not welded?

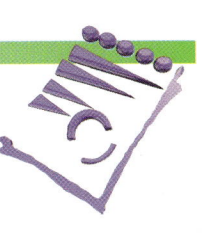

**Key words**

weld
solder
alloy
tin
lead

## 24.3 Filling a gap!

Teeth are made of the hardest substance in the human body. It is called **enamel**. If you look after your teeth they will last a lifetime. The trouble is we eat too many sugary foods and this leads to **decay**. Dentists drill out the decayed part of the tooth and fill the gap with an alloy.

- *How many fillings have you got?*
- *Do you usually have an injection before a filling?*

Teeth are usually filled with an alloy containing **mercury**. Alloys containing mercury are called **amalgams**. The dentist's assistant mixes silver, copper and other metals with mercury to make a paste. Some new fillings use materials called **composites**. A composite is a material that contains two or more different substances. The composite used for fillings contains **silica powder** and a **resin**. The resin acts like a glue and sets to make a tough filling.

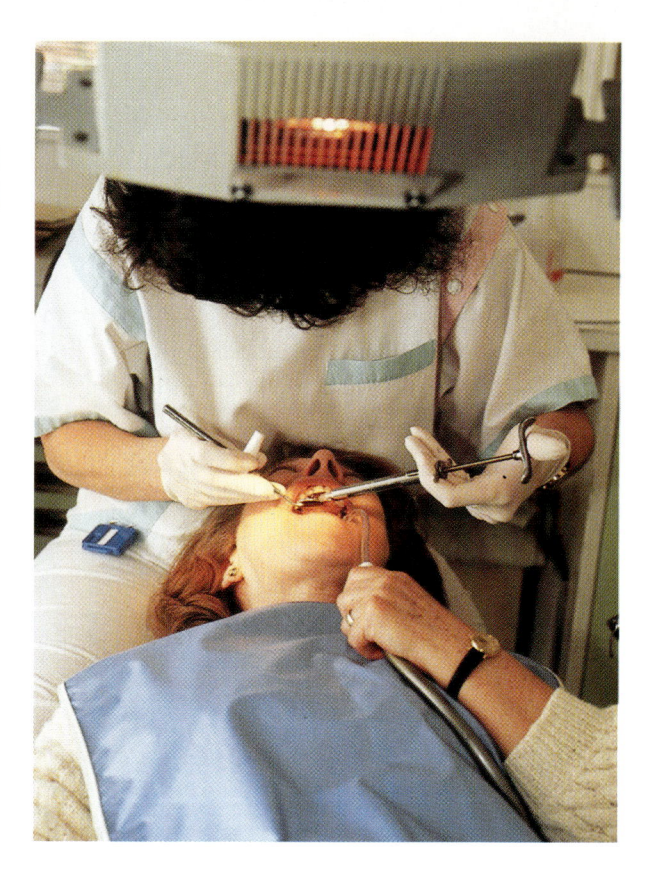

| Mercury amalgam | Silica-resin composite |
|---|---|
| Silver-grey colour | Matched to the tooth colour |
| Contains mercury which is harmful | Contains no mercury |
| Can produce allergies | No known allergies |
| Filling has to be wedged into hole | Filling is bonded to the remains of the tooth |
| Can be used for filling large holes | No good for large holes |
| Quick to do | Slower to do |
| Cheaper than composite materials | More expensive than amalgams |

1. What name is given to a mixture of metals containing mercury?
2. Write down three advantages of new composite materials for filling teeth.
3. Write down three disadvantages of new composite materials for filling teeth.
4. Plan a test to find out how easily a material for filling teeth can be broken. If you can, carry out your test on samples of plaster or concrete.

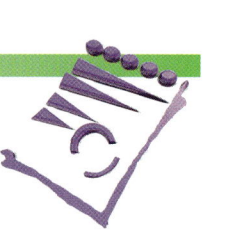

**Key words**

enamel
decay
mercury
amalgam
composite
silica powder
resin

## 24.4 It's a racket!

Tennis players can now hit a ball so hard it travels at over 100 mph! Get in the way of one of those serves and you could get something worse than a black eye!

- Have you ever played tennis?
- Do you own a tennis racket? What is it made of?

The top speed of a tennis serve has been going up over the last few years. Is this because the players are getting stronger or is it something to do with their tennis rackets?

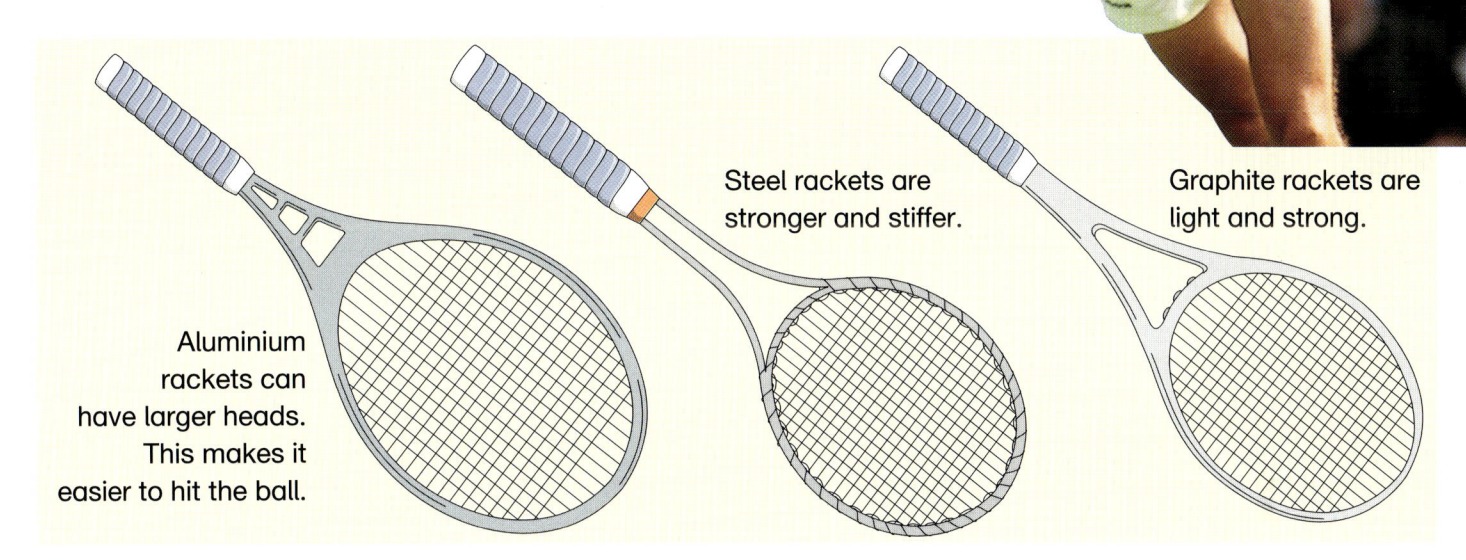

Aluminium rackets can have larger heads. This makes it easier to hit the ball.

Steel rackets are stronger and stiffer.

Graphite rackets are light and strong.

| Material | Density / g per cm$^3$ | Strength (1 = weakest) | Does it rust? |
|---|---|---|---|
| Wood | 0.7 | 3 | no |
| Aluminium alloy | 2.8 | 8 | no |
| Steel | 7.8 | 6 | yes |
| Graphite | 1.9 | 15 | no |

1. Which material is the strongest?
2. Give two advantages of graphite over steel for making a tennis racket.
3. Draw a bar chart to show the differences in strength of the materials in the table.
4. Plan an investigation to find out how the surface on which a ball bounces affects the height of the bounce.

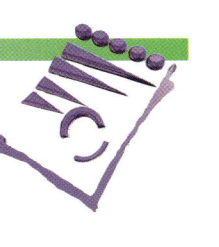

**Key words**

density
graphite

# 25 Trapped underground

## 25.1 Sediments

These men have just been rescued from a cave system that they were exploring.

- Would you ever fancy doing some cave exploration or even being part of a cave rescue team?
- What do you think it would be like in a cave?
- What would you take with you if you went caving?

**Limestone** is a **sedimentary** rock. It is made when the remains of tiny creatures or other chemical deposits settle out of water. **Sandstone** and **mudstone** are also sedimentary rocks. They all form in layers from small particles. It can take millions of years to make a metre of sedimentary rock.

As rainwater trickles through the rocks it reacts with the limestone, making cracks and caves.

Limestone is often used for statues and building stone, because it is easily available, easy to work and looks attractive. Unfortunately, acid rain **reacts** with the stone and it crumbles away.

1. Give two examples of sedimentary rock.
2. Explain how sedimentary rock forms.
3. Why is limestone often used for building work?
4. What is the problem with using limestone for statues and buildings?
5. Explain, using diagrams, how caves are made.

**Key words**

limestone
sedimentary
sandstone
mudstone
react

## 25.2 Minerals and crystals

Digging for diamonds is dangerous. It's also a dirty job. Diamonds are expensive because they are rare and beautiful. They are formed very deep in the Earth where it is very hot and the rocks are under great pressure.

- Why do you think people risk their lives searching for diamonds?
- Would you like to work in a diamond mine? Why? Why not?

A **mineral** is any chemical in a rock. Different minerals form **crystals** that are different shapes and colours. Rocks which have formed slowly have large crystals. You can grow crystals yourself by leaving mineral **solutions** in a warm place. The crystals grow as the water **evaporates**. Some hard minerals are used for making jewellery. Most minerals don't look like crystals at all.

A diamond is a very hard mineral. If something is hard it will scratch anything that is less hard. Glass cutters use a very hard blade to scratch glass. Then they can snap the glass cleanly along the scratch.

1. What is a mineral?
2. Explain how you could grow some mineral crystals at home.
3. How would you find out whether glass was harder than clear plastic?
4. Give two reasons why diamonds are so expensive.

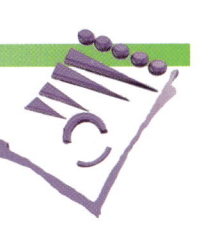

**Key words**

mineral
crystal
solution
evaporate

## 25.3 Earthquake!

Earthquakes happen when layers of rock move past each other. Earthquakes can cause a lot of damage. Many people have been killed when buildings have collapsed on them.

- What might you notice during an earth tremor?
- What is your school built of?
- Do you think it could survive an earthquake?

Buildings may be built of various materials, for example wood, bricks and concrete. **Bricks** are made from **clay** baked hard in the oven. **Concrete** is made from sand, **cement** and small stones. Concrete can be made stronger (reinforced) by putting metal rods into it.

Movements of rocks can produce a fault. One side may move up, the other down.

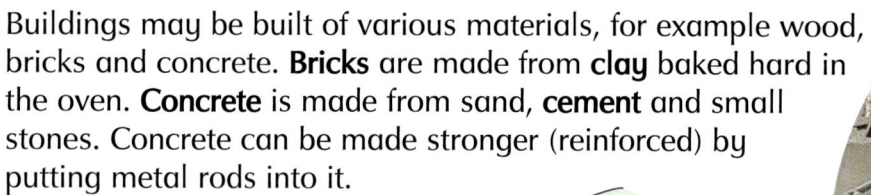

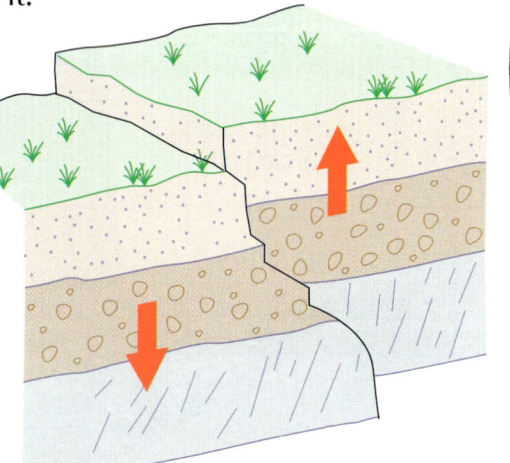

Rocks that have been under the surface of the Earth for many thousands of years may be exposed during earthquakes. The heat and pressure from movement of the rocks underground can be enormous. This forms a new kind of rock called **metamorphic** rock. Heat and pressure can change limestone into marble. Marble is a metamorphic rock.

1. List the advantages of wood, clay and concrete for building homes.
2. List the disadvantages of wood, clay and concrete for building homes.
3. How may concrete be reinforced?
4. What do geologists call rocks that have been changed under heat and pressure?
5. Give an example of a metamorphic rock.

**Key words**

brick
clay
concrete
cement
metamorphic

## 25.4 Volcanoes

The inside of the Earth is so hot that the rocks melt. A volcano is a place on the surface of the Earth where hot, melted rock comes out. Dust, smoke and large lumps of solid rock often erupt from volcanoes too. Volcanoes may lie **dormant** for many years, but then they suddenly **erupt**.

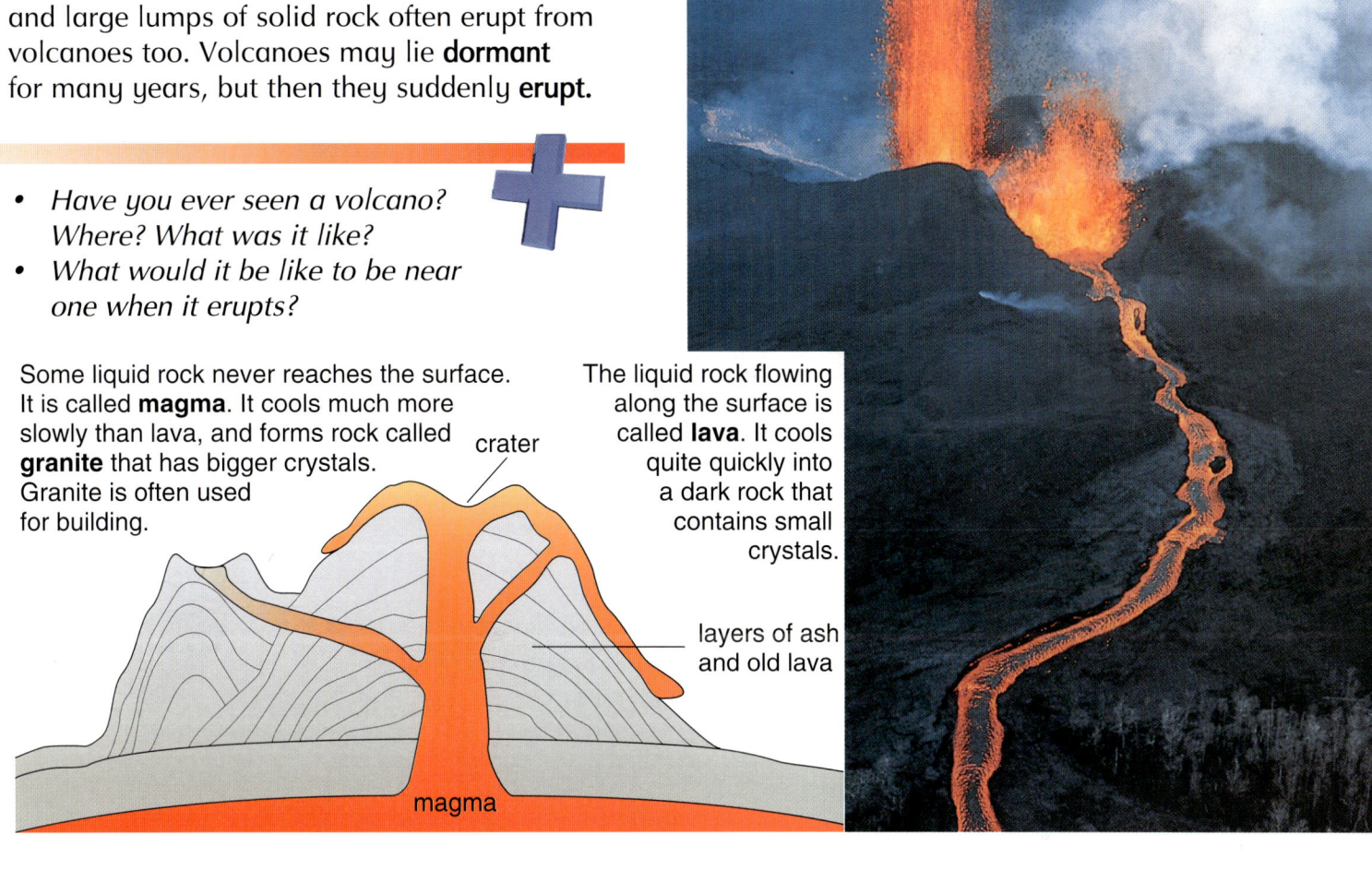

- Have you ever seen a volcano? Where? What was it like?
- What would it be like to be near one when it erupts?

Some liquid rock never reaches the surface. It is called **magma**. It cools much more slowly than lava, and forms rock called **granite** that has bigger crystals. Granite is often used for building.

The liquid rock flowing along the surface is called **lava**. It cools quite quickly into a dark rock that contains small crystals.

crater

layers of ash and old lava

magma

Rocks that come from volcanoes are called **igneous** rocks.

The surface of the Earth is made of a number of pieces called plates. These plates move around at a speed of a few centimetres per year. Earthquakes and volcanoes are common along the edges of the plates. They are rare in the middle of the plates.

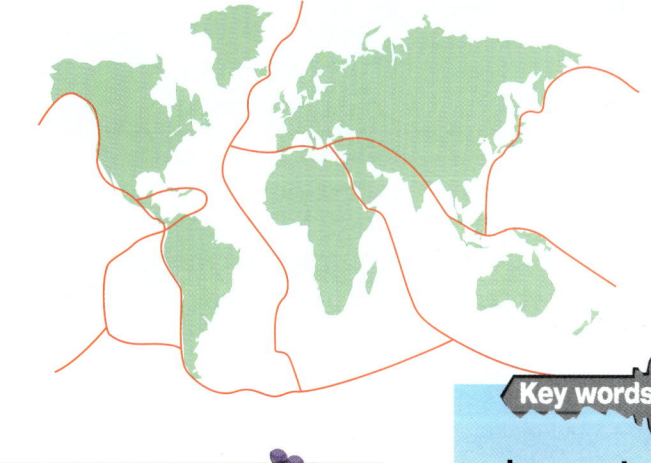

1. What is an igneous rock?
2. Why do some igneous rocks have large crystals in them?
3. What is the difference between magma and lava?
4. Why are there no volcanoes or major earthquakes in Britain?

**Key words**

dormant
erupt
lava
magma
granite
igneous

## K5 Antiques roadshow?

*I found a dusty old vase in our attic while I was clearing out ready to move. It did not look valuable. In the move it was damaged – a pity, because the vase was an antique worth over £2000! I tried to repair it but it is never as good as new. I suppose it's now worth about £800.*

- Have you ever found anything worth a lot of money?
- Finders keepers; losers weepers. Do you think this is fair with buried treasures? Why?

**Restoring** antiques can be very tricky. Just a simple job like sticking a handle on an old mug can be difficult. You must choose the right **glue** – and you can't test glues on **expensive** antiques.

| Glue | Useful for | No good for |
| --- | --- | --- |
| Wallpaper paste | Sticking paper and cardboard | Plastics, metals |
| Superglue | Paper and cardboard, some plastics and metals, pottery | Some plastics |
| Wood glue | Wood, paper and cardboard | Metals and plastics |
| Plastic model cement | **Polystyrene** models | Paper and cardboard, metals |

1. Which glue is best for sticking paper and wood?
2. Plan an investigation to find out the best glue to stick **crockery**. Once your teacher has checked your plan, carry it out.
3. Use a word processor to write up your investigation.
4. Prepare an illustrated instruction sheet to help people decide on the best glue for a particular task.

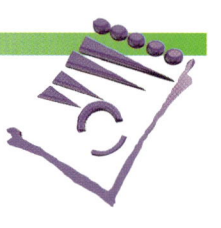

**Key words**

restore
glue
expensive
polystyrene
crockery

# K6 Keeping fit

You don't stop exercising because you get old – you get old because you stop exercising! I run a fitness club for the over-fifties at our local leisure centre. We get over a hundred people coming to sessions during the week. Tumbletots is a group for small kids – less than three years old! It's good for the mums too – the kids work off some of their energy while mum has a coffee and a moment's peace!

- *When did you last get any exercise?*
- *Do you think you get enough exercise?*

Make sure you note down when you do the survey and say who you are. You can tick the responses you get and count up the scores later.

| Name _____ | Date _____ |

**How often do you visit the leisure centre?**

| 1 | 2 | 3 | 4 | 5 | 6 | 7 | 8 | 9 | 10 |
|---|---|---|---|---|---|---|---|---|---|

more than once a week

once a week

less often than once a week

**Which facilities do you usually use?**

| 1 | 2 | 3 | 4 | 5 | 6 | 7 | 8 | 9 | 10 |
|---|---|---|---|---|---|---|---|---|---|

gym

swimming pool

squash courts

1. Find out what is available at your local leisure centre.
2. Design a **survey** to find out who uses your local leisure centre.
3. Collect the **data** and display it in a way that shows when the centre is most busy.

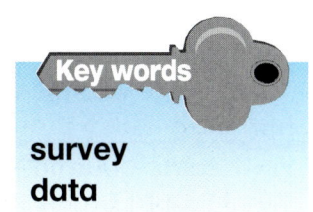

**Key words**

survey
data

# 26 How fast? How slow?

## 26.1 Reactions

A bonfire is a giant **chemical reaction**. The things on the bonfire **react** with oxygen in the air. We call this reaction burning or **combustion**. The faster the reaction the better the bonfire.

- Where was the last bonfire you saw?
- How well was it burning?
- How could you make it burn better?

Not all chemical reactions happen at the same speed. Some are very fast, others take a long time. Sometimes we try to change the speed of reactions.

Some gravestones crumble faster than others. What can affect the speed at which gravestones crumble?

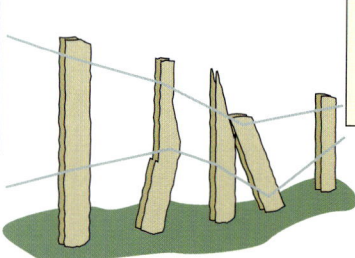

What can you do to slow down the rotting of the fence?

How can you slow down the speed at which milk will turn sour?

These iron pots are thousands of years old. Rusting is a chemical reaction.

1. What is the chemical name for the reaction we call burning?
2. How could you make a bonfire burn more brightly?
3. What stops the bonfire burning in the end?
4. List some very fast chemical reactions.
5. List some very slow chemical reactions.

**Key words**

chemical reaction
react
combustion

38

## 26.2 Alien blood!

In the film *Alien* the monster has **acid** for blood. This makes it very difficult to kill. Any damage to the alien will release acid which will eat its way through the metal hull of the spaceship.

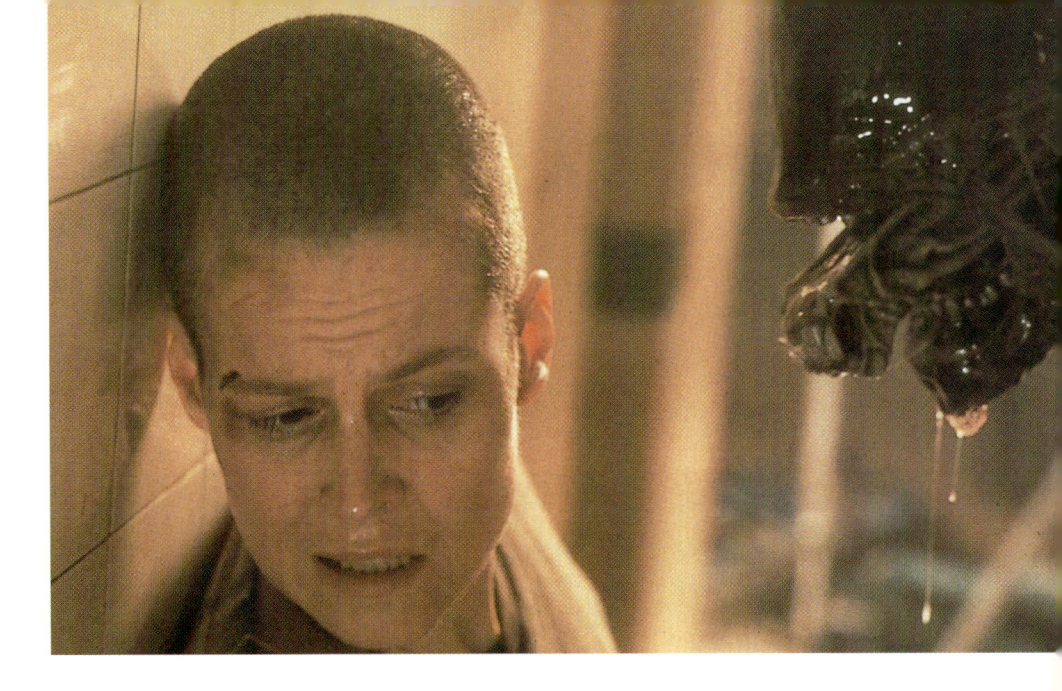

- Science fiction films often have impossible things in them. Do you think this matters?
- What is the strangest thing you have ever seen in a science fiction film?

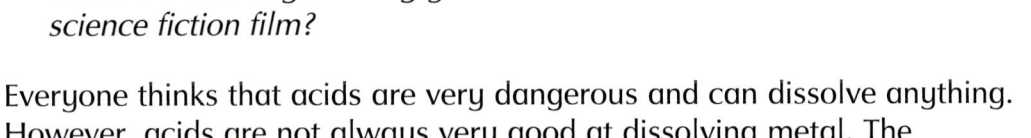

Everyone thinks that acids are very dangerous and can dissolve anything. However, acids are not always very good at dissolving metal. The **reaction** between the acid and the metal can be quite slow. The results below show how quickly zinc dissolves in dilute hydrochloric acid.

Table 1. The metal is added as a large lump.

| Acid | Metal / g | Time to dissolve / secs |
|---|---|---|
| Dilute | 10 | 20 |
| Concentrated | 10 | 13 |

Table 2. The metal is added as a fine powder.

| Acid | Metal / g | Time to dissolve / secs |
|---|---|---|
| Dilute | 10 | 12 |
| Concentrated | 10 | 5 |

1. Which conditions dissolve the metal quickest?
2. What is the longest time taken in the results to dissolve 10 g of metal?
3. How does using powder instead of lumps affect the speed of the reaction?
4. List two ways to speed up the reaction between the acid and the metal.

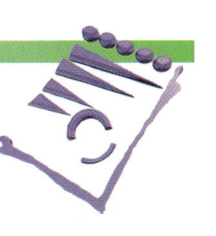

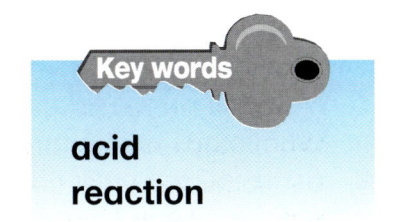

**Key words**

acid
reaction

## 26.3 Setting hard

This car may look better than a modern box but older vehicles often come with dents and scratches. What can car enthusiasts do to keep their cars as smart as possible?

- Would you like to drive one of these cars or would you prefer a modern one?
- What do you think is the most important feature of a car?

The pack of filler has two tubes. One is a large tube of **resin**. The other is a small tube of hardener which contains a **catalyst**. The hardening of the resin is a **chemical reaction**. It is normally very, very slow. The catalyst **speeds up** the setting reaction. Other catalysts can speed up other reactions. Changing the **temperature** can affect the rate of the reaction as well.

| Hardener in 100 g of mixture / g | Time for paste to set / mins |
|---|---|
| 20 | 14 |
| 40 | 10 |
| 60 | 12 |

| Temperature / °C | Time for paste to set / mins |
|---|---|
| 10 | 30 |
| 20 | 12 |
| 30 | 10 |
| 40 | 6 |

Flatten the dent as much as possible with a hammer.

↓

Clean the area around the dent with wire wool.

↓

Mix up the filler paste to the correct recipe.

↓

Fill the dent with the paste and smooth it down.

↓

Let the paste dry. Sand it down and then paint it over.

1. What effect does heating have on the setting time?
2. What effect does using more hardener in the mixture have on the setting time?
3. Would anything happen to the resin if it was left for ten minutes without mixing with the hardener?
4. It says on the pack that you should not mix more than you can use in ten minutes. Why?

**Key words**

resin
catalyst
chemical reaction
speeds up
temperature

## 26.4 Enzymes

Munich has one of the largest beer festivals in the world! In 1996 over 50 thousand visitors downed nearly a million litres of beer (and maybe just a few headache pills!). Good fun or dangerous?

- Do you think you ought to be a certain age before you are allowed to drink alcohol? Why? What age?
- What other laws should we make to control drinking alcohol?

Beer, and all alcoholic drinks, depend on **yeast**. Yeast is alive. Yeast uses **catalysts** to speed up **reactions**. The catalysts in living organisms are called **enzymes**.

Enzymes mean living things can carry out all sorts of reactions at low temperatures. The reactions in yeast produce **alcohol** and **carbon dioxide** from sugar. The enzymes will not work if the temperature is too hot or too cold. Most enzymes work best at around 30–35°C.

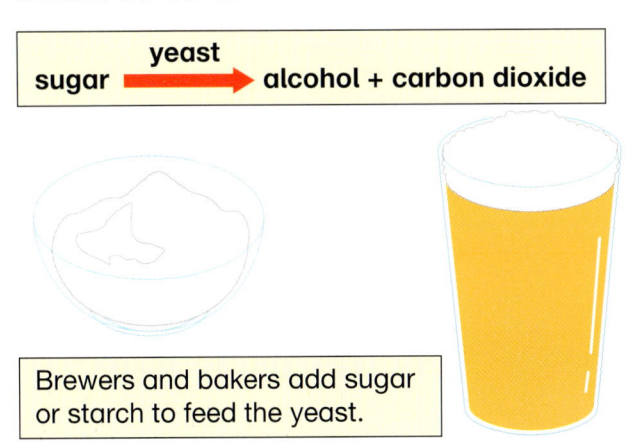

sugar →(yeast)→ alcohol + carbon dioxide

Brewers and bakers add sugar or starch to feed the yeast.

Carbon dioxide gives the beer its frothy head. In bread the bubbles of carbon dioxide are trapped in the dough. They make the dough rise.

Alcohol makes you drunk if you drink too much beer. In bread the cooking drives off the alcohol.

1. What are enzymes?
2. What substances are produced when yeast acts on sugar?
3. Cooks leave bread dough to rise in a warm place before cooking it. Why?
4. How does the gas made when enzymes act on starch or sugar improve the bread or beer?

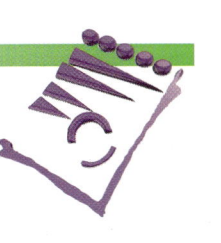

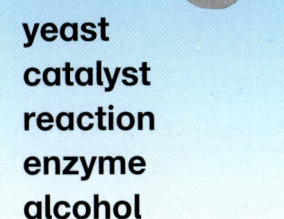

**Key words**

yeast
catalyst
reaction
enzyme
alcohol
carbon dioxide

# 27 Sorting out

## 27.1 Getting the gold

This man spends most of his life sorting through wet mud. The chances of finding real gold are pretty small – but if he does he will be rich. Gold dust is very heavy. It is left in the machine when he washes the less heavy rock away with water.

- What would you be willing to do for money?
- Would you like to search for gold? Why?

**Mixtures** may contain substances that are useful. To get the useful substance the mixture has to be **separated**. The method of separation depends upon the properties of the substances.

Tea leaves settle to the bottom of the teapot. The liquid tea can then be poured off the top. This method of separating a solid from a liquid is called **decanting**.

A tea bag is made of a material that lets water through but not the tea leaves. The tea bag acts as a **filter**.

1. Write a sentence that uses the word decant.
2. Gold is much heavier than rock. Explain how this helps people to find gold dust.
3. Explain how you would get fresh water from sea water.
4. Plan an experiment to get pure salt from rock salt.

**Key words**

mixture
separate
decant
filter

## 27.2 The truth is out there

Every year hundreds of people meet aliens ... perhaps. Some are taken into spaceships. A few even travel to different planets ... maybe.

- Do you think aliens have ever visited the Earth?
- Would you like to meet an alien? Why? Why not?

Some people claim to have an alien document. How could you test to see if it is fake? The ink could be the answer.

Ink is a mixture of **soluble** coloured substances. These can be separated by **chromatography**. Chromatography separates the different colours from the ink mixture so comparisons between samples can be made. If the ink is from an alien spacecraft it should have a different mix to ink from Earth.

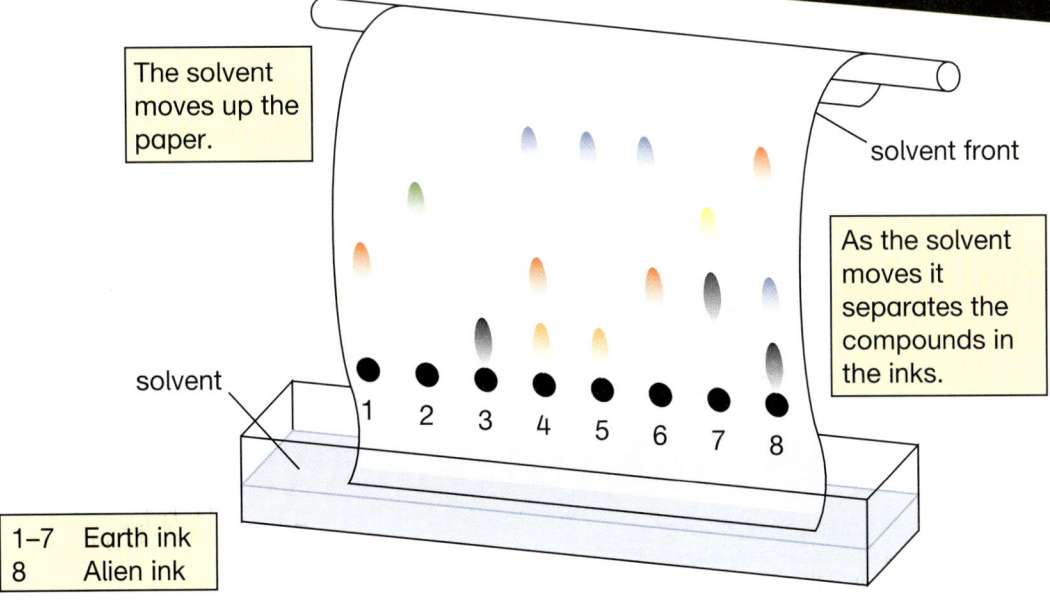

The solvent moves up the paper.

solvent front

As the solvent moves it separates the compounds in the inks.

solvent

1  2  3  4  5  6  7  8

1–7   Earth ink
8     Alien ink

1. Write a sentence that uses the word solvent.
2. Name some substances that could be separated by chromatography.
3. Plan an experiment to find if the colours of Smarties are pure substances or mixtures.

**Key words**

soluble
chromatography
solvent
separate

## 27.3 Cleaning the blood

Blood is a very complex mixture. Medical staff use a range of different techniques to find out what is in blood.

- *Would you like to work in a laboratory in a hospital doing work like this?*
- *Have you ever seen a **centrifuge** or used anything like it?*

To separate cells from the blood doctors use a centrifuge. The centrifuge spins samples of blood around very fast. The cells settle at the bottom of the tube.

Kidney machines use a technique called **dialysis** to wash waste substances from the blood. The blood is pumped along tubes made of a special material. The wastes pass through the material but the rest of the blood cannot. Dialysis solution passing in the opposite direction in the outer tube carries away these wastes. The blood can then go back into the patient.

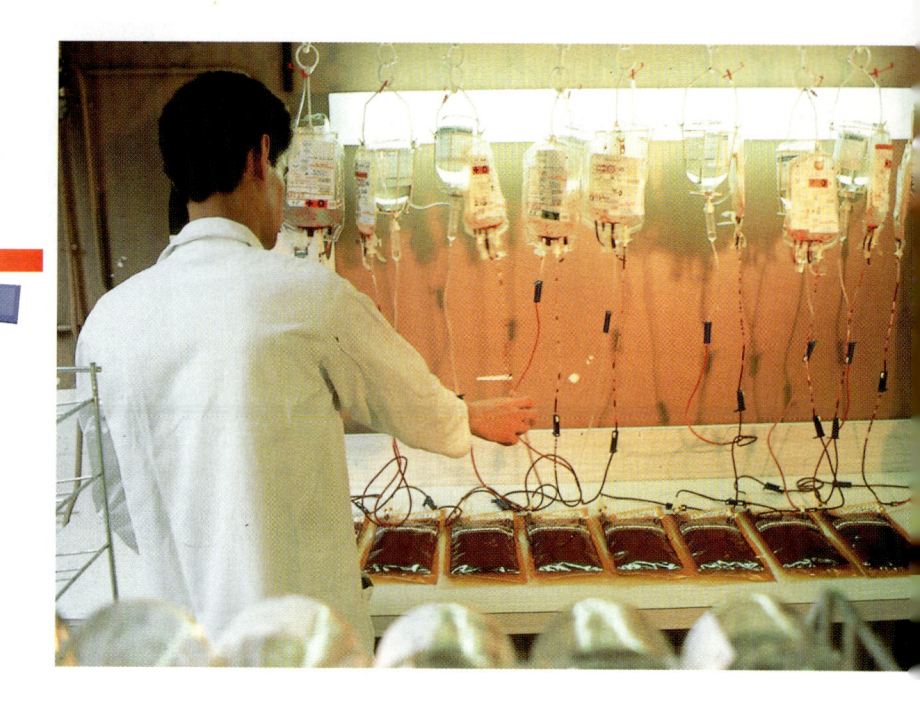

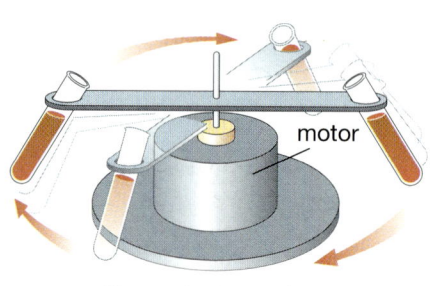

The motor turns the rotary arm very fast.

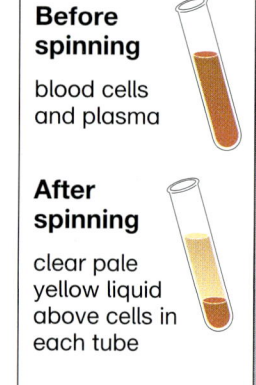

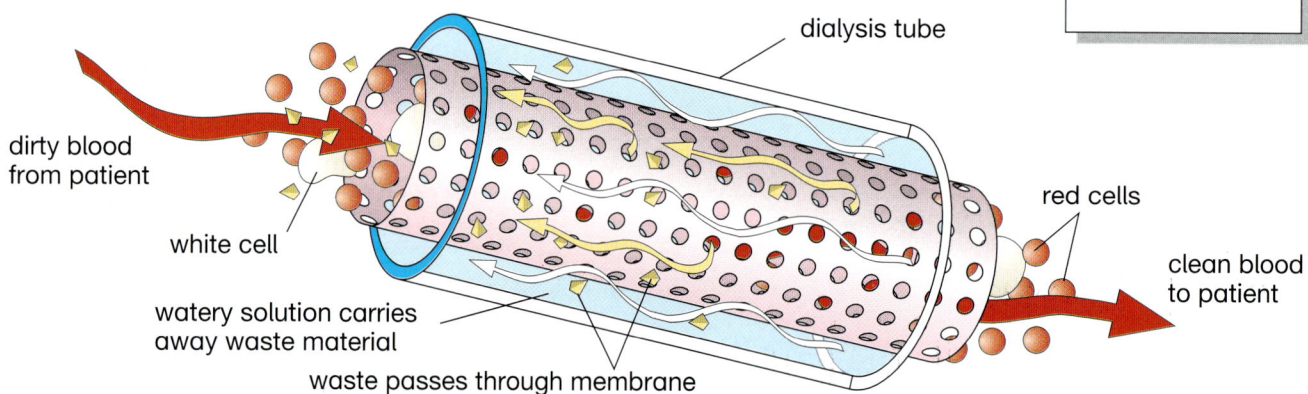

**Before spinning**
blood cells and plasma

**After spinning**
clear pale yellow liquid above cells in each tube

dirty blood from patient
white cell
watery solution carries away waste material
waste passes through membrane
dialysis tube
red cells
clean blood to patient

1. What do hospitals use centrifuging for?
2. Which machine in a hospital uses dialysis?
3. What does this machine do?
4. Design a leaflet to explain to patients how the separation techniques used in hospitals work. Include the separation of blood products and dialysis.

**Key words**

centrifuge
dialysis

## 27.4 Separating liquids

Some liquids mix so well they look like one substance. Many liquid mixtures can be separated by a technique called **distillation**. Whisky makers use the same technique to make whisky.

- Whisky is always served in smaller glasses than beer. Why?
- Moonshine is a kind of whisky made in a homemade still. Why could it be dangerous to drink?

**Crude oil** can be sorted into different liquids by **fractional distillation**. The technique works because different liquids in the mixture have different **boiling points**.

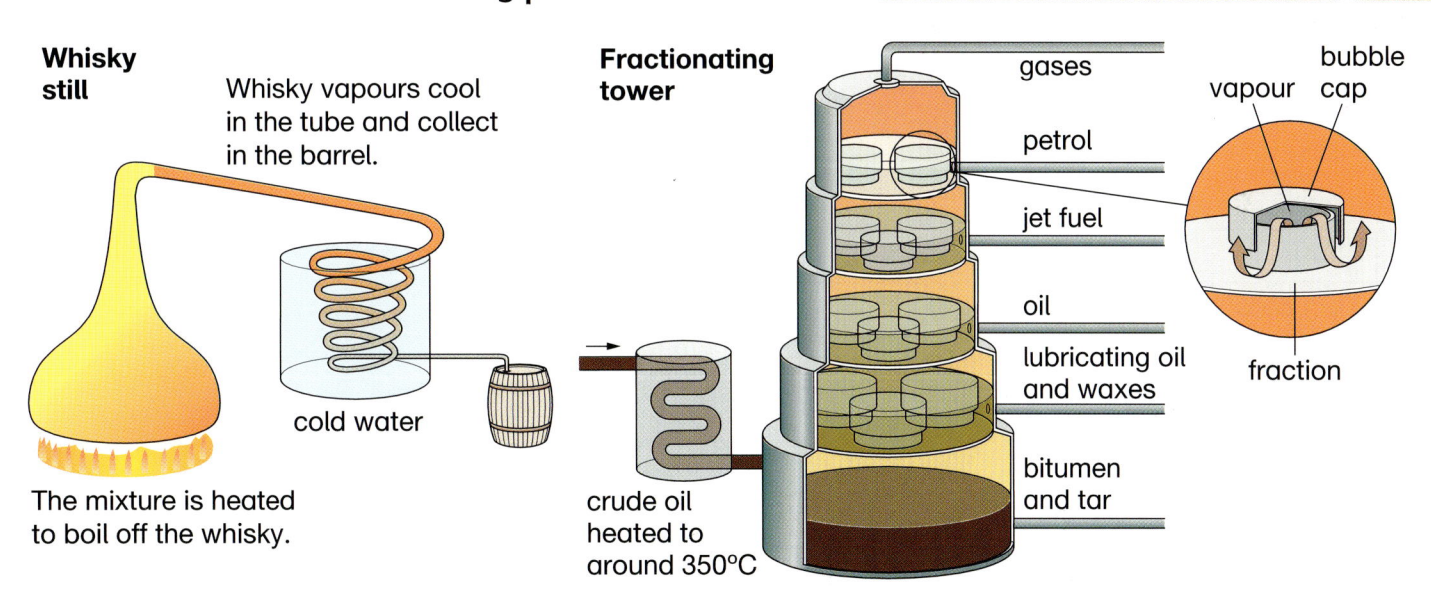

**Whisky still**
Whisky vapours cool in the tube and collect in the barrel.
The mixture is heated to boil off the whisky.

**Fractionating tower**
crude oil heated to around 350°C

gases
petrol
jet fuel
oil
lubricating oil and waxes
bitumen and tar

bubble cap
vapour
fraction

1. Write a sentence containing the word distillation.
2. Name two liquid mixtures that can be separated by fractional distillation.
3. What difference in two liquids does fractional distillation depend on?
4. How could you tell if a perfume is a mixture or a pure liquid?

**Key words**

distillation
crude oil
fractional distillation
boiling point

45

# K7 Survival bags

I work for a company that designs and makes camping equipment. Most of our money comes from tents and rucksacks but we also sell a range of small items like compasses, waterproof matches, sewing kits for campers and so on. We are just about to launch a range of **survival** bags and blankets. I need to know how these work – and how much they cost to make.

- Have you ever been camping? What equipment did you take?
- Were you warm enough at night?
- Do you want to go again?

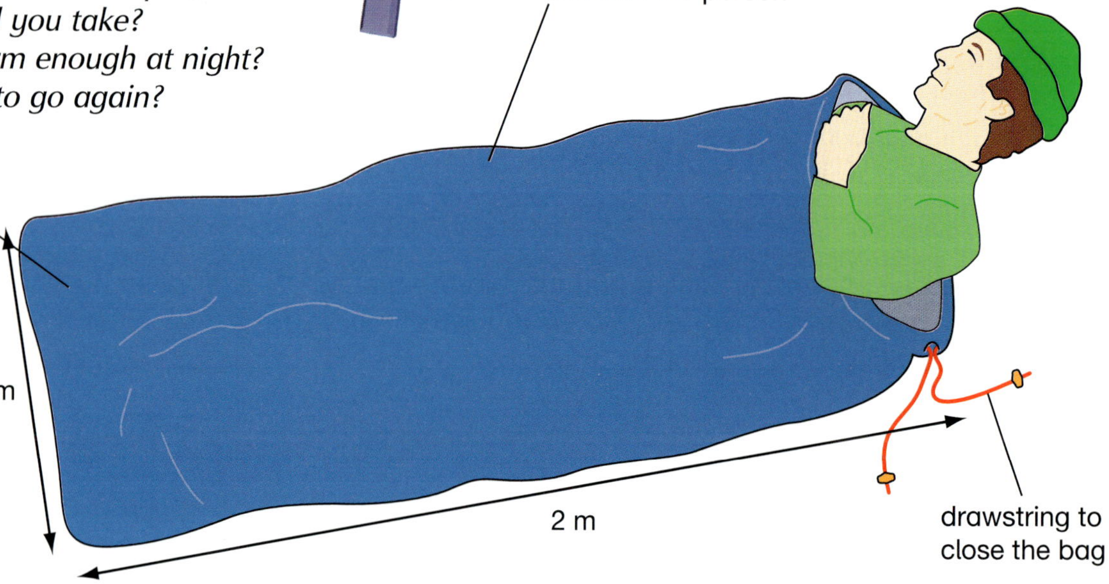

material reflects heat back towards the person

thin fabric, easy to fold so it takes up very little space when not in use

70 cm

2 m

drawstring to close the bag

| Fabric | Cost of fabric / m² | Weight of fabric / g per m² |
|---|---|---|
| Thin **plastic** | 15p | 80 |
| Thick plastic | 35p | 250 |
| **Foil** | 45p | 120 |
| **Metalised** plastic | 50p | 165 |
| Cotton | £1.75 | 400 |

1. Which fabric is the heaviest?
2. Give two reasons why cotton is probably not a good idea for a survival bag.
3. How much would the fabric for one foil survival bag cost?
4. Pick a fabric from the table that you think would make the best survival bag for the company.

**Key words**

survival
plastic
foil
metalised

## K8 Keep it cool!

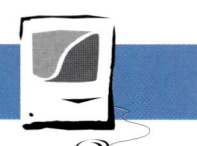

I work for a supermarket chain checking that we give our customers the freshest possible foods. I have to work out the **sell-by** dates for foods that go off quickly like milk and meat and fish. I am looking at ways to keep the milk **fresher** for longer. We normally store milk at about 10°C. How much longer would it last if we kept it colder? Would it be worth the extra cost?

- Why is it so important for the supermarket to keep its food fresh?
- How long do you think a supermarket will keep milk before it is too **sour** to sell?

| Storage temperature / °C | Time until the milk goes off per hour |
|---|---|
| 25 | 4 |
| 20 | 6 |
| 15 | 15 |
| 10 | 24 |
| 5 | 48 |
| 0 | 96 |

| Size | Cost to buy | Cost to run per hour in summer | Cost to run per hour in winter |
|---|---|---|---|
| 200 bottle cabinet | £1100 | £5 | £4 |
| 400 bottle cabinet | £1700 | £7 | £6 |
| 600 bottle cabinet | £2400 | £8 | £7 |

1. How soon would milk go off at a **temperature** of 15°C?
2. Draw a chart to show how temperature affects the speed that milk goes sour.
3. A supermarket sells 300 bottles of milk every day. How much would a cabinet to keep them cool in the shop cost?
4. Why do fridges cost more to run in the summer than in the winter?

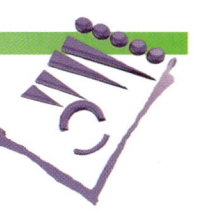

**Key words**

sell-by
fresher
sour
temperature

# 28 Our school's rubbish

## 28.1 Is it all rubbish?

Each of us produces roughly half a tonne of rubbish every year. Some of this really is rubbish – but most could be useful! It could be collected and **recycled** to make new products.

- Do you collect anything for recycling? Why? Why not?
- Does your school collect anything for recycling? Why? Why not?

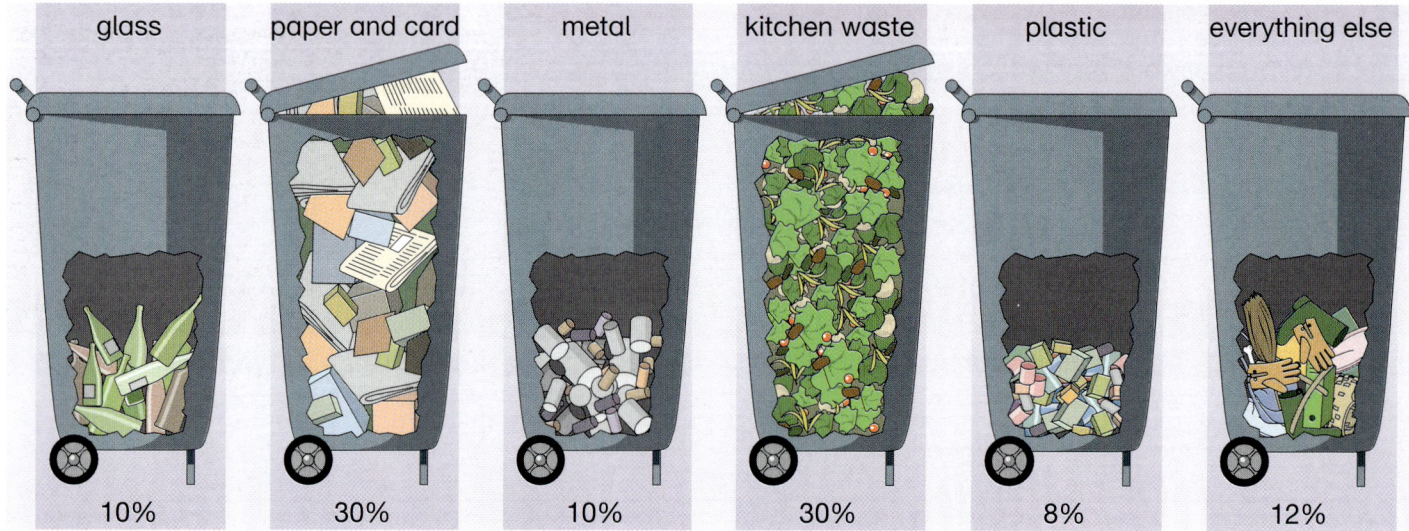

| glass | paper and card | metal | kitchen waste | plastic | everything else |
|---|---|---|---|---|---|
| 10% | 30% | 10% | 30% | 8% | 12% |

The problem with rubbish is that it's such a mixture. All the different parts need to be treated differently. Old food, kitchen waste and paper will **rot** easily. This is called **biodegradable** rubbish. Plastics, glass and metal will not rot. This is called **non-biodegradable** rubbish.

Recycling rubbish means using it to make something useful. This new product could look very different from the rubbish. Waste papers can be recycled to make new paper or furniture or bricks which will burn. Some types of plastic can even be recycled as fleece jackets and tops.

1. Write a sentence containing the word biodegradable.
2. Sort the rubbish in the diagram into things which are biodegradable and those which are not.
3. Draw a diagram to show the amounts of different materials in your rubbish bin at home.

**Key words**

**recycle**
**rot**
**biodegradable**
**non-biodegradable**

## 28.2 What a gas!

Large amounts of the rubbish we make ends up in a hole in the ground. These holes are often old quarries. They are filled up and then covered with soil. They are called **landfill sites**. Who knows – you may be sitting on a landfill site right now!

- What finishes up in the bins or skip at your school?
- How often is the rubbish collected from your school?

Landfill may sound like a good idea. The rubbish is covered up and out of the way. However, we are running out of holes to fill. Another problem is that the biodegradable rubbish can start to **rot**. **Methane** gas rises through the soil and can collect in buildings above ground. A spark can make the methane air mixture explode.

The rubbish is covered up and out of the way.

The biodegradable rubbish starts to rot.

The rubbish makes methane gas. The methane gas can be piped off to use as a fuel.

1. Which gas is made in landfill sites?
2. What must be mixed with this gas before an explosion can take place?
3. What sorts of rubbish give off methane?
4. What sorts of rubbish are safe to bury in landfill sites?

**Key words**

**landfill site**
**rot**
**methane**

## 28.3 Burning rubbish

Burying rubbish is a waste of **energy**. We will never run out of rubbish. In fact, each year we produce more and more. Rubbish is called a **renewable fuel**. Two bins of rubbish contain the same energy as one bag of coal.

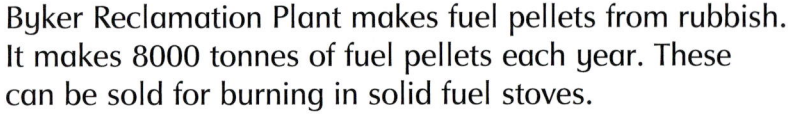

- Which do you think is better – burying rubbish or burning it? Why?
- Would you be willing to sort your rubbish into different bins for burning?

Byker Reclamation Plant makes fuel pellets from rubbish. It makes 8000 tonnes of fuel pellets each year. These can be sold for burning in solid fuel stoves.

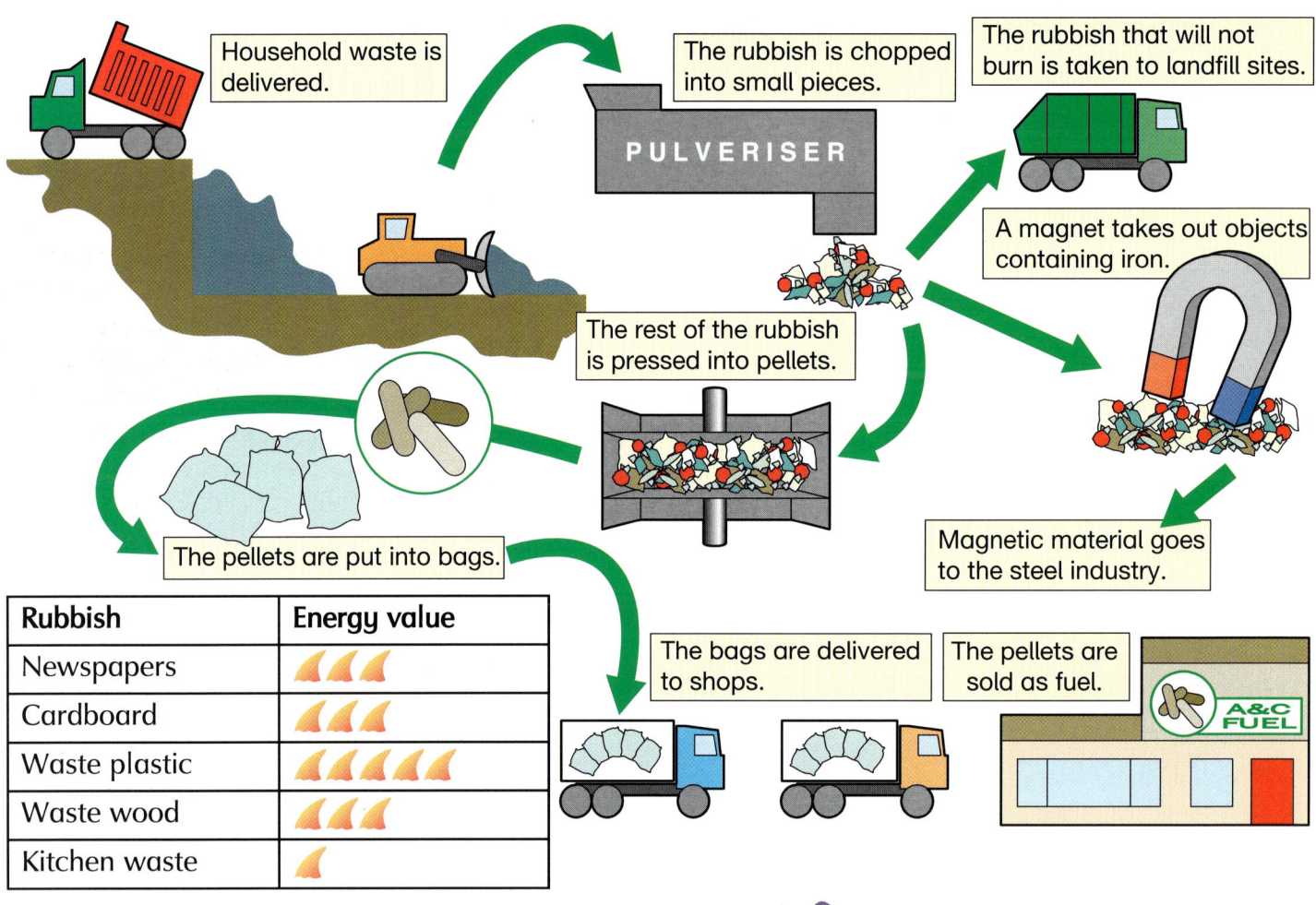

Household waste is delivered.

The rubbish is chopped into small pieces.

PULVERISER

The rubbish that will not burn is taken to landfill sites.

A magnet takes out objects containing iron.

The rest of the rubbish is pressed into pellets.

Magnetic material goes to the steel industry.

The pellets are put into bags.

| Rubbish | Energy value |
|---|---|
| Newspapers | 🔥🔥🔥 |
| Cardboard | 🔥🔥🔥 |
| Waste plastic | 🔥🔥🔥🔥🔥 |
| Waste wood | 🔥🔥🔥 |
| Kitchen waste | 🔥 |

The bags are delivered to shops.

The pellets are sold as fuel.

1. Write a sentence using the word renewable.
2. Sort this list into things which can be used to make fuel pellets and those which cannot.
   cardboard   china   cloth   glass   metals   paper   plastic
3. Draw a bar chart to show the energy in different types of rubbish.

**Key words**

energy
renewable fuel

50

## 28.4 Different fuels

This person is checking on the levels of chicken litter in the hopper. The mixture of dried straw and manure is burnt to provide energy to make electricity. Any ideas why he is wearing a gas mask?

- Which fuels do you use at home?
- Could you start to use rubbish pellets in your home?

There is plenty of coal in the ground and it gives out lots of heat when it burns.

We ought to look at other ways to heat our homes. What about wind or water power? At least they won't run out.

Natural **gas** burns well and is clean.

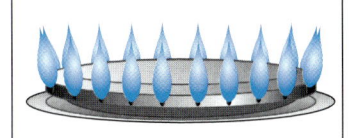

Oil is a good fuel – but we ought to be careful how much we use. It will not last forever.

Rubbish pellets solve the problem of landfill sites by giving us something useful. But when they burn they still give out **ash** and **smoke**. This is an important type of **pollution**.

1. List some sources of energy that will never run out.
2. Make a list of the advantages of using rubbish pellets as fuel.
3. Now list some of the disadvantages of using rubbish pellets as fuel.
4. Draw a design for a stove that would be able to use rubbish pellets as fuel. Show how it is different from a gas stove.

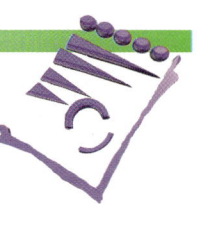

**Key words**

gas
ash
smoke
pollution

# 29  Who needs energy?

## 29.1  Sources and uses

- What do you use **energy** for at home?
- Where does the energy come from to light and heat your school?
- Where does the energy come from which makes vehicles move?

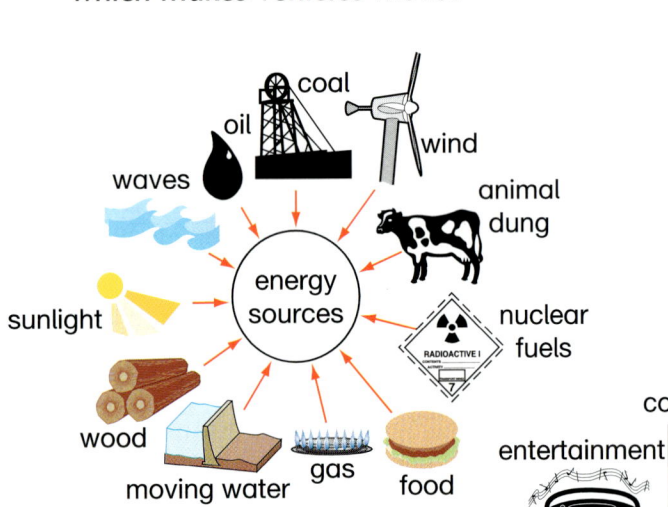

Energy is needed to get things done. Energy makes people and **machines** work. We get our energy from different **sources**. People get their energy from the food they eat. Machines get energy from **fuel** or electricity. Some farms in Australia have their own electricity **generators** which run on oil or wind power. In North Africa they use wood and animal dung for fuel.

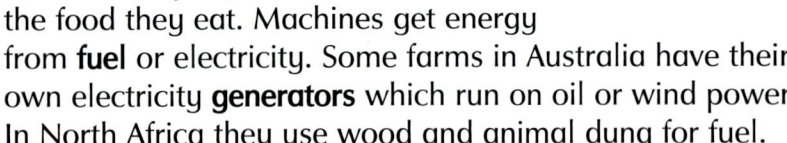

1. List the energy sources mentioned on this page.
2. Sort the list into those you use and those you do not use.
3. Why is bottled gas useful for campers?
4. Why do you think there are no gas or electricity supplies to remote areas?

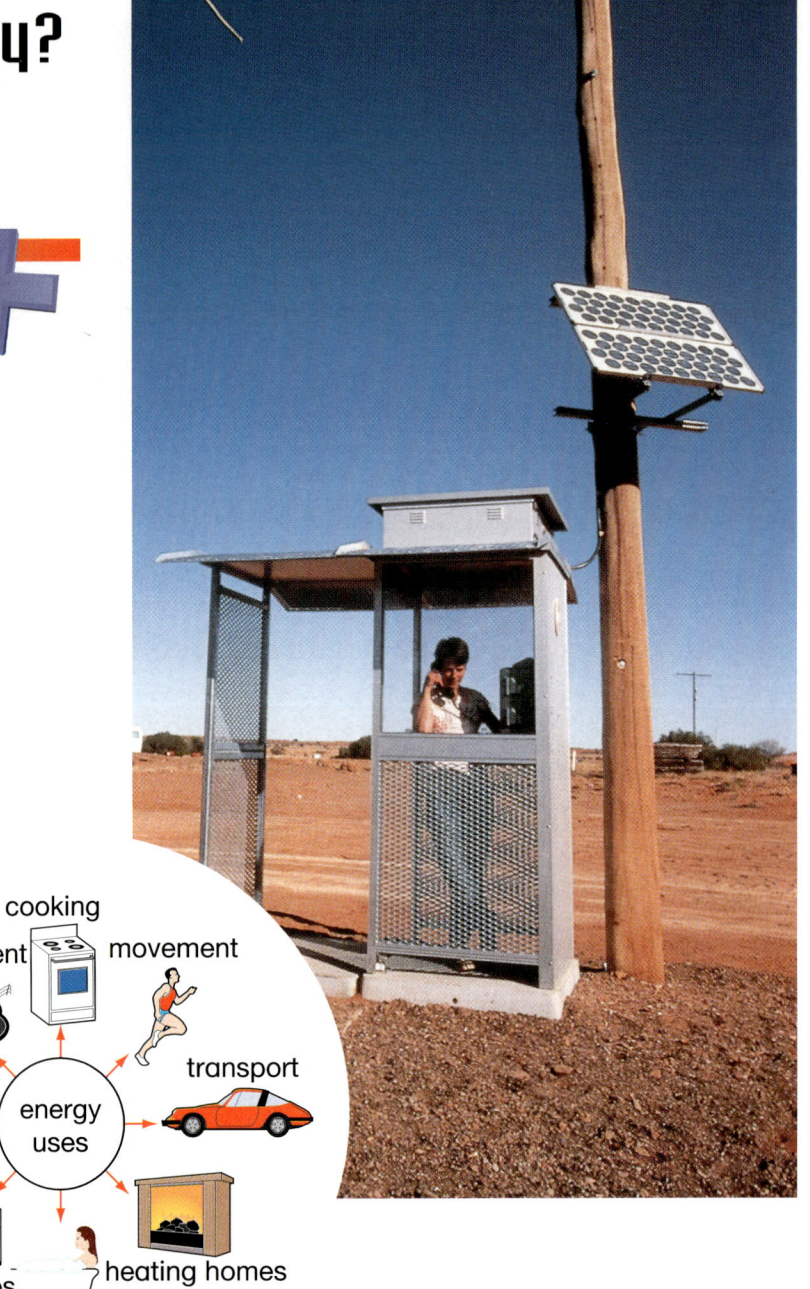

**Key words**

energy
machine
source
fuel
generator

## 29.2 Non-renewable energy sources

- Which fuels do you burn at home?
- How easy is it to light a barbecue?
- Describe a fire or explosion caused by burning fuels. You may have seen one on TV or in a film.

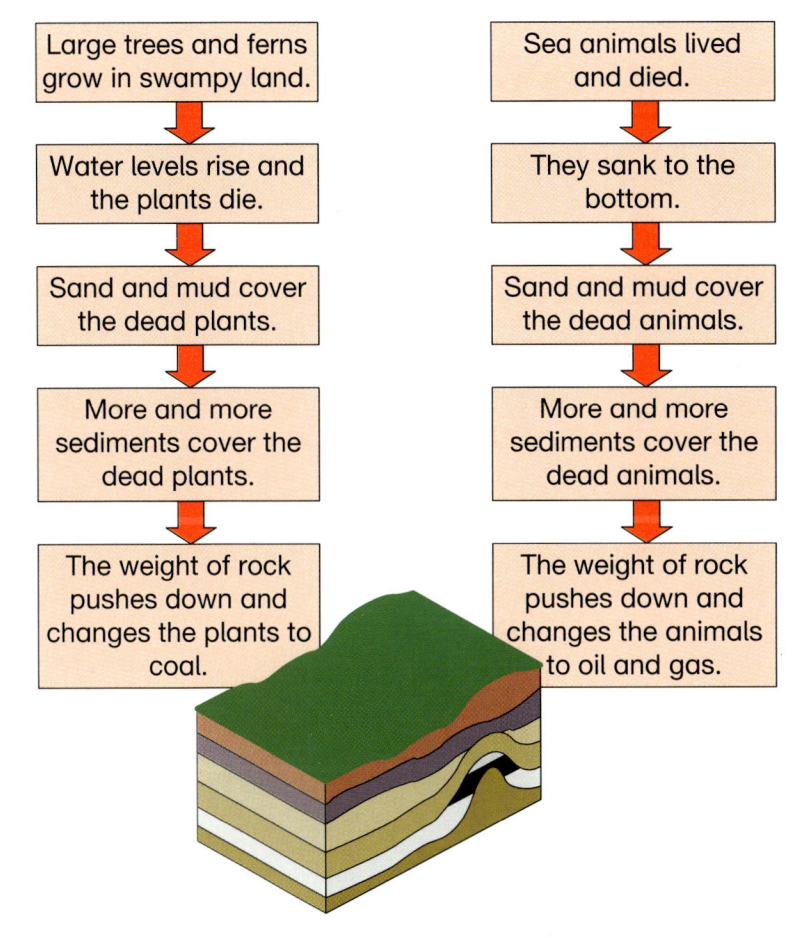

| Large trees and ferns grow in swampy land. | Sea animals lived and died. |
| --- | --- |
| Water levels rise and the plants die. | They sank to the bottom. |
| Sand and mud cover the dead plants. | Sand and mud cover the dead animals. |
| More and more sediments cover the dead plants. | More and more sediments cover the dead animals. |
| The weight of rock pushes down and changes the plants to coal. | The weight of rock pushes down and changes the animals to oil and gas. |

Coal, oil and gas were made millions of years ago. They are called **fossil fuels**. They are useful because they release **energy** when they burn. **Uranium** is another fuel that is found underground. We use it in nuclear power stations to make electricity. No more fossil fuels or uranium will be made. Fuels which cannot be replaced are called **non-renewable** fuels. Eventually we will run out of non-renewable fuels.

1. Write a sentence containing the word non-renewable.
2. List the non-renewable fuels on this page.
3. Sort them into fossil fuels and nuclear fuels.
4. Which non-renewable fuels can be used in the home?
5. Why can burning fuel be bad for the environment?

**Key words**

**fossil fuel**
**energy**
**uranium**
**non-renewable**

## 29.3 Renewable energy sources

- Have you got a calculator that does not use batteries? Where does it get its **energy**?
- Have you ever seen or been in a sailboat? Where did it get its energy?

We can get energy from the wind, waves, tides and the sun. None of these energy sources will run out as long as the Earth exists. These are **renewable** energy sources. The sun can be used directly to heat things and the wind can be used to turn machinery. Most renewable energy sources are used to make **electricity**. Renewable energy sources do not make **pollution**. Collecting the energy can be expensive and take up a lot of space. Wind turbines are very noisy.

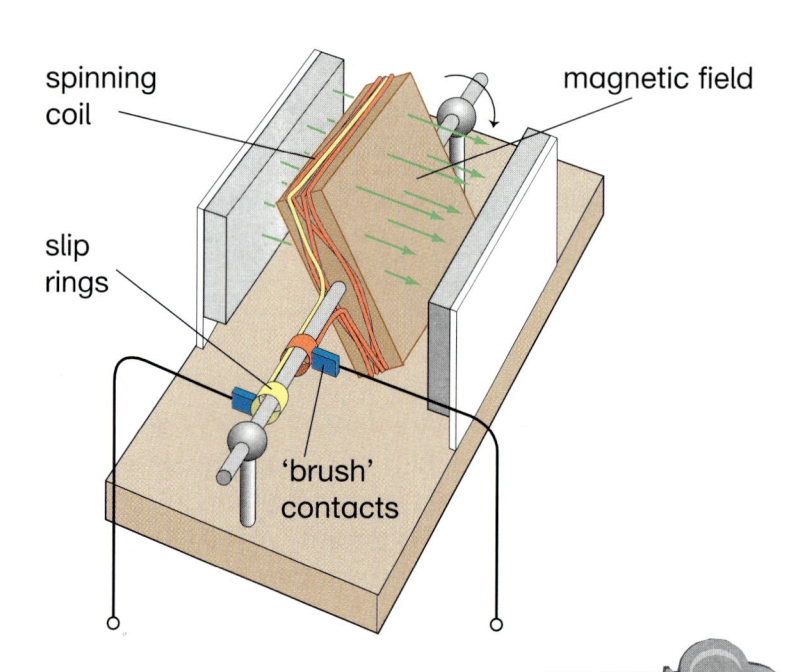

spinning coil
magnetic field
slip rings
'brush' contacts

1. List some renewable energy sources.
2. What do you use in school which is run on **solar power**?
3. What can be made from renewable energy sources?
4. List the advantages of renewable energy sources.
5. Give some disadvantages of renewable energy sources.

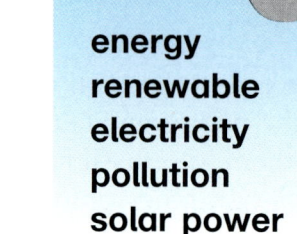

**Key words**

energy
renewable
electricity
pollution
solar power

## 29.4 Waste not, want not

A great deal of the heat in a house escapes and heats the air outside instead. This is a **waste** of energy and money. Energy transfers from hot places to cold places. Stopping heat escaping is called **insulation**.

- Does your house stay warm long after the heating has been switched off?
- Is your loft insulated?
- Do all the houses in the photo have loft insulation? How can you tell?

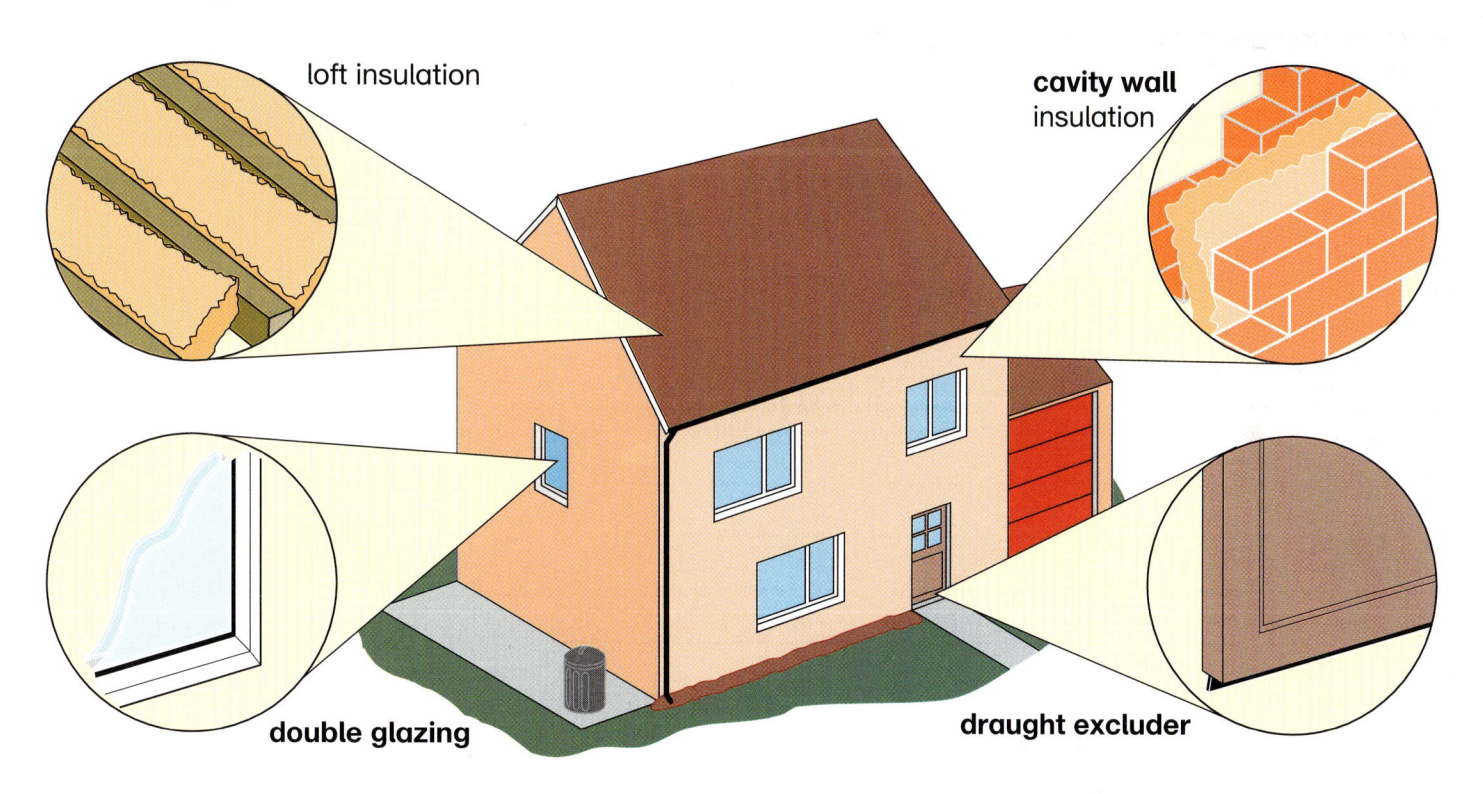

loft insulation

cavity wall insulation

double glazing

draught excluder

1. List the things that people can do to cut down energy loss from their homes.
2. Put the list in order starting with things which save the most energy.
3. If you had to choose only one method for your house which would you choose and why?

**Key words**

**insulation
cavity walls
double glazing
draught excluders**

## K9 Cooking times

No-one likes **soggy**, over-cooked vegetables! I need to know exactly how long it takes to cook **vegetables** so that they are ready when people want them. And I have to have everything else ready at the same time.

- What things might affect how **quickly** vegetables cook?
- Why else is it important not to over-cook vegetables?

| Food | Rough cooking times / mins |
| --- | --- |
| Carrots (sliced) | 10 |
| Peas (from frozen) | 5 |
| Steak (medium) | 15 |
| Chips (from frozen) | 15 |
| Tomatoes (grilled) | 3 |

1. How long does it take to cook carrots?
2. I want the chips and the peas to be ready at the same time. Which vegetable should I start cooking first?
3. How long before the steak is ready should I put the chips on to cook?
4. Prepare a **flow chart** to show when you need to do things to cook the meal in the picture.
5. Plan an investigation to find out if the thickness of the carrot slices affect how long they take to cook.

**Key words**

soggy
vegetables
quickly
flow chart

# K10 Dog's dinner

I work for a large **pet food** manufacturer. I have to feed the dogs in the kennels with our newest foods to see how they affect their growth. I need to know exactly how much of each food type I give these dogs.

- Have you got any pets? What sort?
- How do you know if they are getting a healthy diet?

**Food 1 — Percentage composition**
- Protein 7.5
- Oil 5.0
- Ash 2.0
- Fibre 0.2
- Moisture 85.3

**Food 2 — Percentage composition**
- Protein 8.2
- Oil 5.5
- Ash 2.0
- Fibre 0.3
- Moisture 84.0

| Size of dog | Approximate weight of the dog / kg | 400 / g cans needed per day | Biscuits and mixer added per day / g |
|---|---|---|---|
| Small | 5–10 | 1 | 400 |
| Medium | 10–30 | 2 | 800 |
| Large | 30–50 | 3 | 1200 |

1. How much **oil** does a can of Food 1 contain?
2. How much **protein** is there in Food 2?
3. Joe has three small dogs and one medium one to feed with Food 1. Work out how many cans he will need.
4. How much protein would a large dog eat in one day?

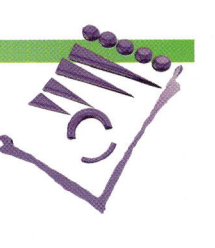

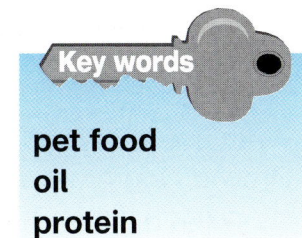

**Key words**

pet food
oil
protein

# 30 In the balance

## 30.1 Chain gang

Moving boulders isn't easy! You can break them into smaller blocks and carry them ... or you can use a **lever**.

- Have you ever had to move a very heavy load?
- What tools do you use? What for?

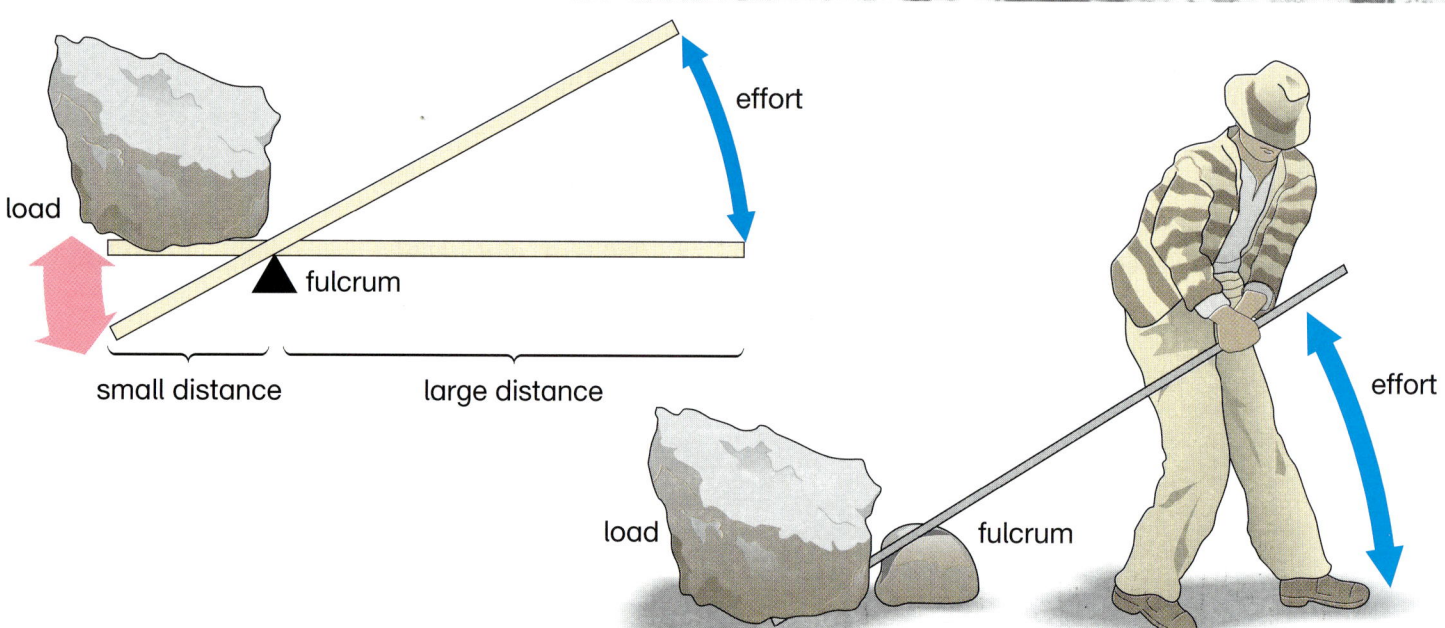

*effort*

*load*

*fulcrum*

*small distance* — *large distance*

*load*  *fulcrum*  *effort*

A lever is a machine that has a **pivot** or **fulcrum** in the middle. When you use a lever, it turns about the fulcrum. The thing you are trying to move or lift is called the **load** and the force you are using is called the **effort**.

1. What is a lever?
2. Draw a diagram of a lever to explain the terms load, effort and fulcrum.
3. Draw two levers that are used in gardens. Label the load, effort and fulcrum in each one.

**Key words**

lever
pivot
fulcrum
load
effort

58

## 30.2 Big Frank

The weight of boxers is very important because this decides who they are allowed to fight. A super-heavyweight would easily win against a flyweight!

- *Do you think boxers should be sorted by weight into different classes? Why?*
- *Would you take up boxing as a hobby? As a job? Why?*

One sort of weighing machine used for boxers depends on a **balance**. The boxer stands on one side of the balance. A movable weight is on the other side. The weight can be moved closer to or farther away from the **pivot**. When the beam balances the weight on both sides is equal.

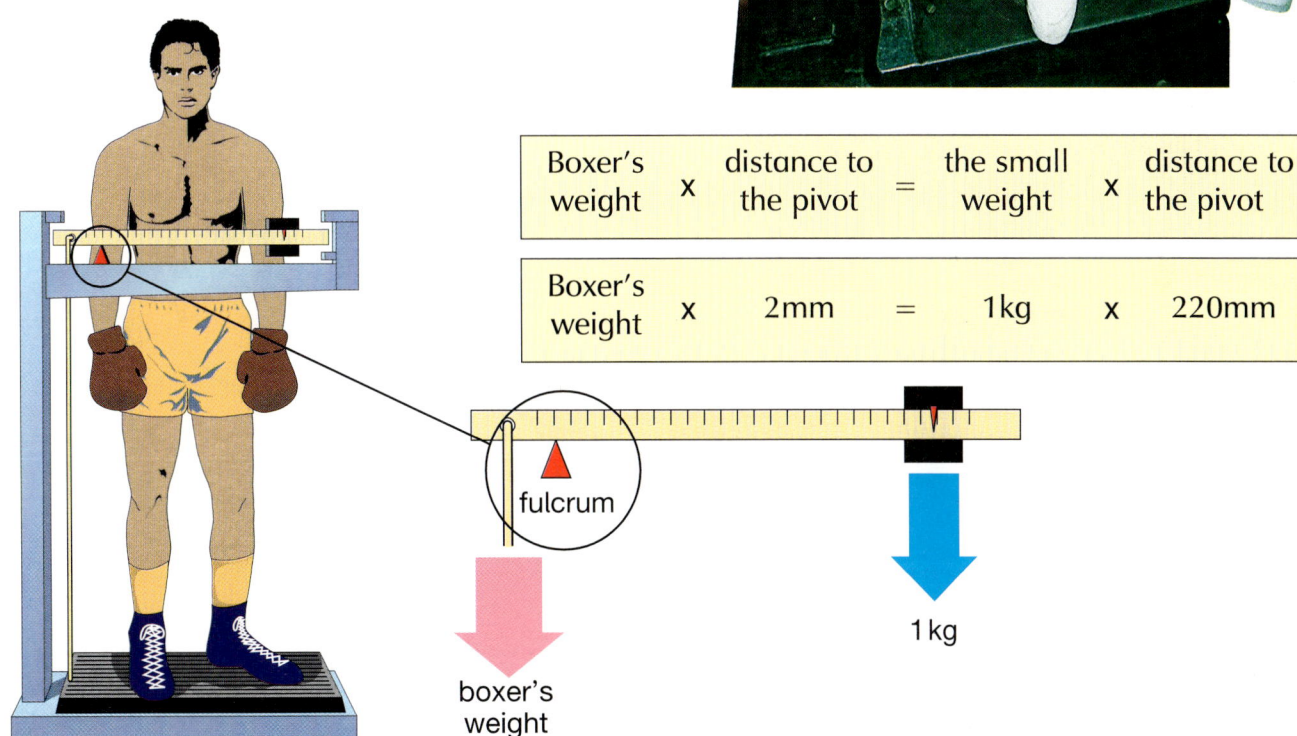

| Boxer's weight | x | distance to the pivot | = | the small weight | x | distance to the pivot |

| Boxer's weight | x | 2mm | = | 1kg | x | 220mm |

fulcrum

boxer's weight

1 kg

1. Work out Frank's weight using the figures above.
2. Design a balance to weigh out sugar in a kitchen.
3. Design a seesaw for a park. It must be safe and allow children of different weights to play on it.

**Key words**
balance
pivot

## 30.3 Well balanced

If you choose the wrong vase and it tips over you can end up with a nasty mess. We say that something is **stable** if it is hard to knock over. Things that are stable usually have wide bases. They often have heavy bases too. This means that most of their **mass** is low down.

- List some things that are specially made so that they are stable.
- Why is it important that these things do not fall over?

What is the easiest way to carry a ladder? When the ladder is **balanced** it feels as if all its mass is in one place, just above your shoulder. This point is called the **centre of mass** of the ladder. Some people use the words **centre of gravity**. This means the same as centre of mass. Anything will balance if you support it at its centre of mass.

1. Write a sentence containing the word stable.
2. Why do vases often have wide, heavy bases?
3. Why is a ladder easier to carry if you support it in the middle?
4. Design a set of glasses for the restaurant car on the Orient Express train. The tables wobble as the train moves, so the glasses need to be very stable.

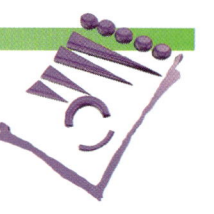

**Key words**

stable
mass
balance
centre of mass
centre of gravity

# 30.4 Bridges

- *Would you walk across this bridge?*
- *Have you ever crossed streams using bridges that don't seem very safe?*

These bridges are made from different materials and to different designs. However, they all do a similar job. The **pillars** of the bridges carry the **weight**. The **arches** make sure the weight acts through the pillars.

1. Draw some designs for some bridges.
2. Pick one of your designs and build a model of it.
3. Plan an investigation to find out the strength of your bridge. Once your teacher has checked your plan, carry it out.
4. Use the results from your investigation to improve the strength of your bridge.

**Key words**

pillars
weight
arch

# 31 Music machines

## 31.1 The concert

The band uses so many instruments. The **sound** is very loud. You can feel the **beat** of the music in your stomach.

- Have you ever been to a concert or disco? How loud was it?
- Can you play a musical instrument? Would you like to?

We make sounds in many different ways. They all depend on transferring energy. The more energy the louder the **volume**. The energy is carried by **vibrations**. These vibrations can travel through gases, liquids or solids.

cymbal, piano, drums, guitar, horn, saxophone, double bass

1. Make a list of musical instruments.
2. Sort your list into stringed instruments, wind instruments and drums.
3. Plan an investigation to find out how changing the length of a plucked string changes the note. If you can, carry out your investigation.

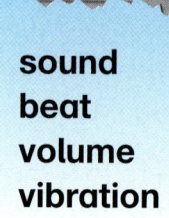

**Key words**

sound
beat
volume
vibration

62

## 31.2 The recording studio

Every band wants to cut its first single. With luck it goes on to fortune and fame. Most don't make it though!

- Would you like to play in a band?
- What would you say if your friends told you they were leaving their jobs to set up a band?

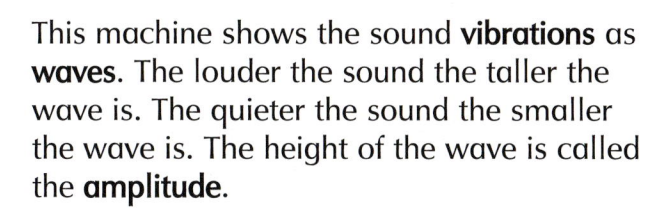

This machine shows the sound **vibrations** as **waves**. The louder the sound the taller the wave is. The quieter the sound the smaller the wave is. The height of the wave is called the **amplitude**.

The machine also shows how high or low **pitched** the note is. If the note is low pitched the wave is long. If the note is high pitched the wave is short. This is called the **wavelength** of the wave. The **frequency** is the number of wavelengths that you can fit into one second. Notes with a long wavelength have a low frequency. Notes with a short wavelength have a high frequency.

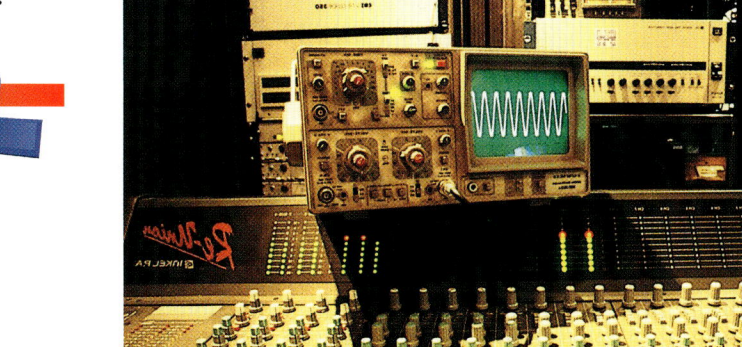

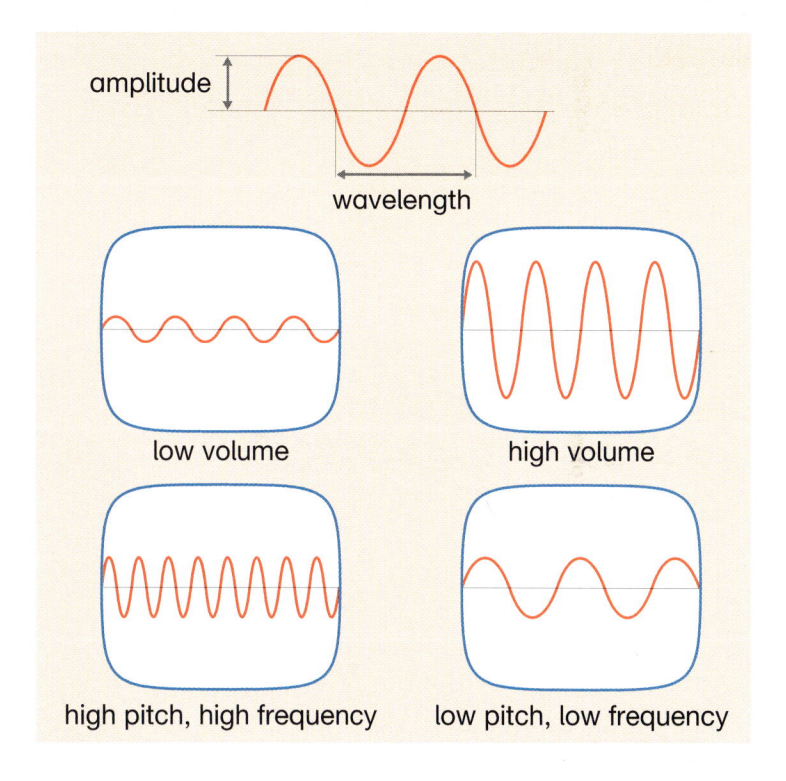

1. Draw a wave. Label it with the words amplitude and wavelength.
2. The recording studio invites school groups to visit. Make a leaflet for pupils that explains what they will see.
3. Draw some high frequency soundwaves.
4. If you were told that you had a high pitched voice what would that mean?

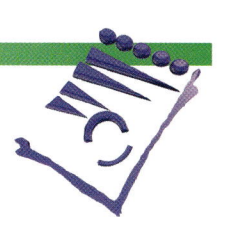

**Key words**

vibration
wave
amplitude
pitch
wavelength
frequency

## 31.3 Whale song

You can buy recording of dolphins and whales making noises. People claim listening to them helps them to relax – some parents use them to help their babies sleep.

- *Some people think dolphins speak to each other. Do you agree? Why?*
- *Would you like to swim with a dolphin in a pool? Why? Why not?*

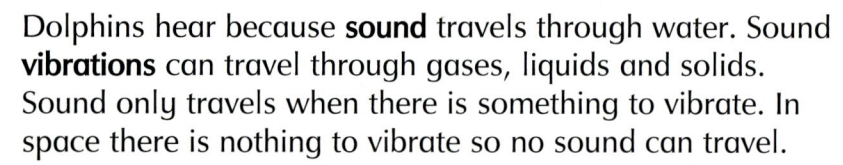

Dolphins hear because **sound** travels through water. Sound **vibrations** can travel through gases, liquids and solids. Sound only travels when there is something to vibrate. In space there is nothing to vibrate so no sound can travel.

Soundwaves can be reflected. We call this an **echo**. Sounds **reflect** best from hard surfaces. Bats use this to judge distances and ships use **echo sounding** to find the depth of the sea.

Depth of sea = 1/2 time x speed of sound in water

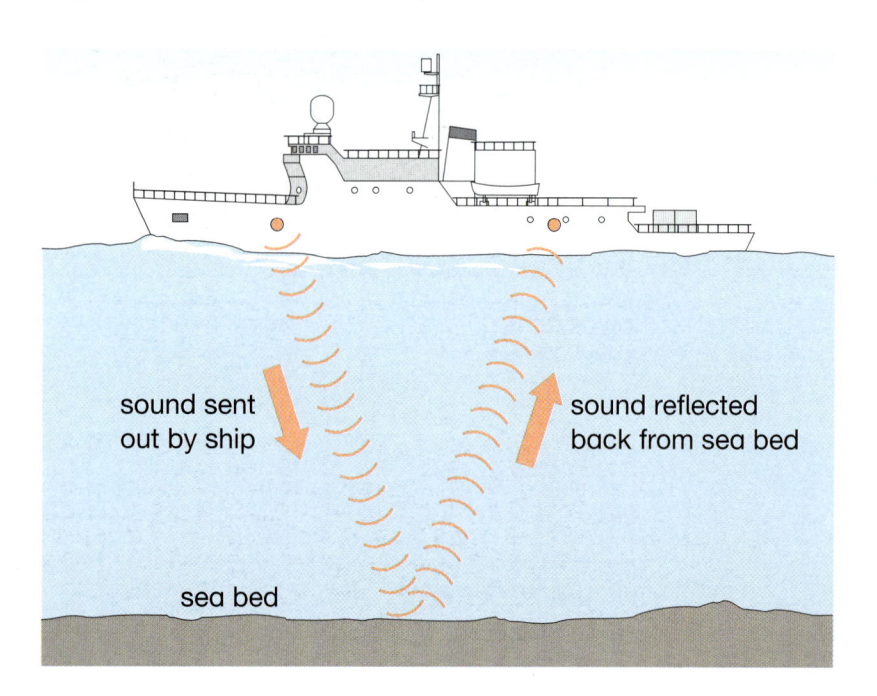

| Substance | Speed of sound / m per sec |
|---|---|
| Air | 330 |
| Water | 1500 |
| Steel | 5170 |

sound sent out by ship

sound reflected back from sea bed

sea bed

1. What is an echo?
2. A ship is using echo sounding to find the depth of the sea. The ship sends out a sound and receives the echo after two seconds. Calculate the depth of the sea. How deep would the sea be if the time was four seconds?
3. Plan an experiment to measure the speed of sound in air.
4. Why does sound seem louder in the bathroom than in the living room?

**Key words**

**sound**
**vibration**
**echo**
**reflect**
**echo sounding**

## 31.4 Ears

Many people listen to music that is too loud. They go to pop concerts and use personal stereos at full volume. Some of them will suffer from ringing in their ears and permanent ear damage.

- Have you ever had a hearing test? What happened?
- Have you ever had a very bad cold? What happened to your hearing?

Very loud sounds can be harmful. After listening to loud music it takes time for your ears to recover. If the sounds are too loud for too long the damage can be permanent. Noise pollution is monitored by environmental officers. They can confiscate the source of **noise pollution**, so if someone always plays music too loud they can lose their equipment.

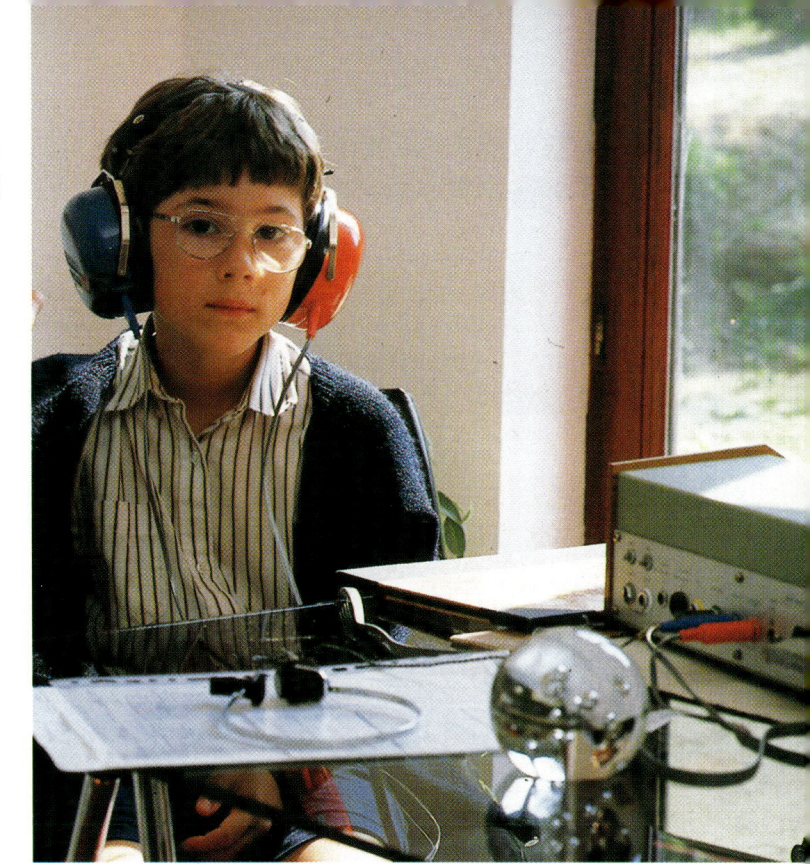

**Tiny bones**
These three tiny bones carry the vibration of the eardrum across to the liquid in the inner ear.

**Cochlea**
A coiled tube that converts vibrations to **nerve impulses**.

**Inner ear**
In the inner ear sounds are changed into nerve signals.

**Outer ear**
Sound waves are collected into the funnel-shaped outer ear.

**Auditory nerve**
This carries impulses to the brain.

**Eardrum**
This vibrates as sound waves hit it.

**Middle ear**
The air-filled space behind the eardrum.

**Eustachian tube**
This connects the middle ear with the back of the mouth. This keeps the air pressure the same on both sides of the eardrum.

1. Design a leaflet to put with new personal stereos to make sure they are used safely.
2. Why should people who work with noisy machines wear ear protectors?
3. Design a poster to show the causes and problems of noise pollution.

**Key words**

noise pollution
eardrum
nerve impulse
eustachian tube
auditory nerve

# K11 Hospital garden

> I design gardens for **hospitals**. For people who are in hospital for very long periods of **treatment** the garden might be the only **outdoor** place they can visit. The first thing is always to talk to the people who will use the garden – what do they want? We start with small groups so that everyone can put in some **suggestions**.

- Have you ever been in hospital for a long time?
- Did you get a chance to go out for some fresh air?

> It would be good to have some grass to sit on – it's much softer than concrete and stone.

> The wind is quite strong here – that can make it quite cold in winter.

> A pond or waterfall is very relaxing. Could we have some goldfish in it as well?

> I use a wheelchair – please make sure there are no steps that I cannot get up.

> It would be nice to have some colourful flowers – just to cheer people up a bit.

> What happens when it rains? Can you add some shelter?

1. Work in a group. List as many ideas for the garden as possible.
2. Sort your list into three groups: good ideas, bad ideas and ones you are not certain about. Try to make the third group as small as possible.
3. Use your good ideas to design the garden.
4. Produce a plan and some drawings to show what your garden would look like. Show your designs to people in another group and explain why you have included the different parts.

**Key words**

hospitals
treatment
outdoor
suggestions

## KS12 Recycle it!

*I work for a voluntary group that collects materials from people's homes every day and sells them on to **recycling** companies. Last year we shifted tonnes of waste paper alone! Of course, all this depends on people giving us their old bottles and newspapers.*

- Do you put your empty bottles in a **bottle bank**? Why? Why not?
- What other materials can be recycled?
- Are there recycling schemes in your area?

Collect the glass – make sure the right colour goes into the right bank!

At the glass factory machines remove tops, lids and other non-glass bits from the broken mixture.

The broken glass is fed into a furnace with fresh raw materials. Over half the mixture going into the furnace could be recycled glass waste. The furnace heats the mixture to 1500°C.

The furnace squirts molten lumps of glass called gobs into metal moulds. The gobs cool to make bottles or jars.

Bottle Bank

1. List the materials that can be recycled.
2. Why is it useful to recycle materials?
3. Design a survey to find out if people nearby would be willing to recycle materials.
4. Find out how much material is available for recycling in your area.
5. Prepare a report to show how much paper and glass you could collect for recycling in your area.

**Key words**

recycling
bottle bank

# 32 Hot stuff

## 32.1 Special effects

Every year hundreds of people are set alight by film directors. These stunt men and women look as though they are burnt to death in thrillers and disaster movies. But they are all safe.

- *Would you like to work as a stunt person in a film? Why? Why not?*
- *Have you ever set fire to something by accident? What happened?*

Things which burn and give out heat are called **fuels**. Fuels can only burn if they get hot enough and there is enough **oxygen**. You can put out a fire if you:
– take away the fuel     – cut off the air supply     – cool it down.

Different methods to put out fires have advantages and disadvantages. Water should not be used on a fat fire because the burning fat will float on the water. Water should not be used for fires caused by electricity. Many fire **extinguishers** have foam inside them. Carbon dioxide may also be used.

1. List the things needed to start a fire.
2. Why shouldn't you use water to put out a fat fire?
3. Make a table that shows the advantages and disadvantages of the different ways to put out a fire.

| Method | Advantage | Disadvantage |

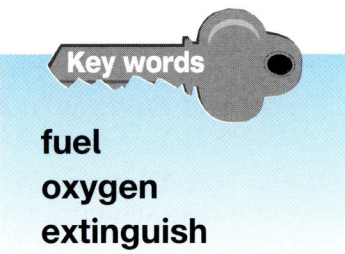

**Key words**

fuel
oxygen
extinguish

## 32.2 Cooking

- What kind of cooker do you have at home?
- What kind of cooker cooks food the quickest?
- How was food cooked before gas and electric cookers were invented?

Some heat from the fire warms the air.

Some heat from the fire goes to the aluminium foil and some goes into the potato.

Some heat from the fire is transferred to the ground.

Some heat goes into the tongs.

Some heat reaches the person.

All cookers transfer heat to food when they cook it. Gas cookers transfer **energy** from the gas as heat energy. Electrical cookers transfer electricity as heat. **Microwaves** use energy in waves to heat food.

Not all of the heat produced by the cooker gets to the food. Some heat warms up the cooker and some escapes into the air. Cookers which transfer most of the energy to the food are **efficient**.

1. How is heat wasted in a gas cooker?
2. List all the ways you could cook a jacket potato.
3. Sort the ways into those which waste a lot of energy and those which do not waste much.
4. Which way of cooking a potato is most efficient?

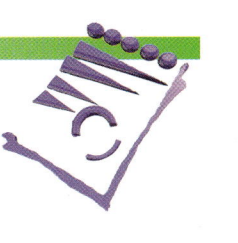

**Key words**

energy
microwave
efficient

69

## 32.3 Keeping food warm

Fast food is more popular than ever. You can buy it in every city centre and shopping mall.

- Which is your favourite take-away food?
- How is your favourite food kept warm?

Plastic is a good insulator of heat.

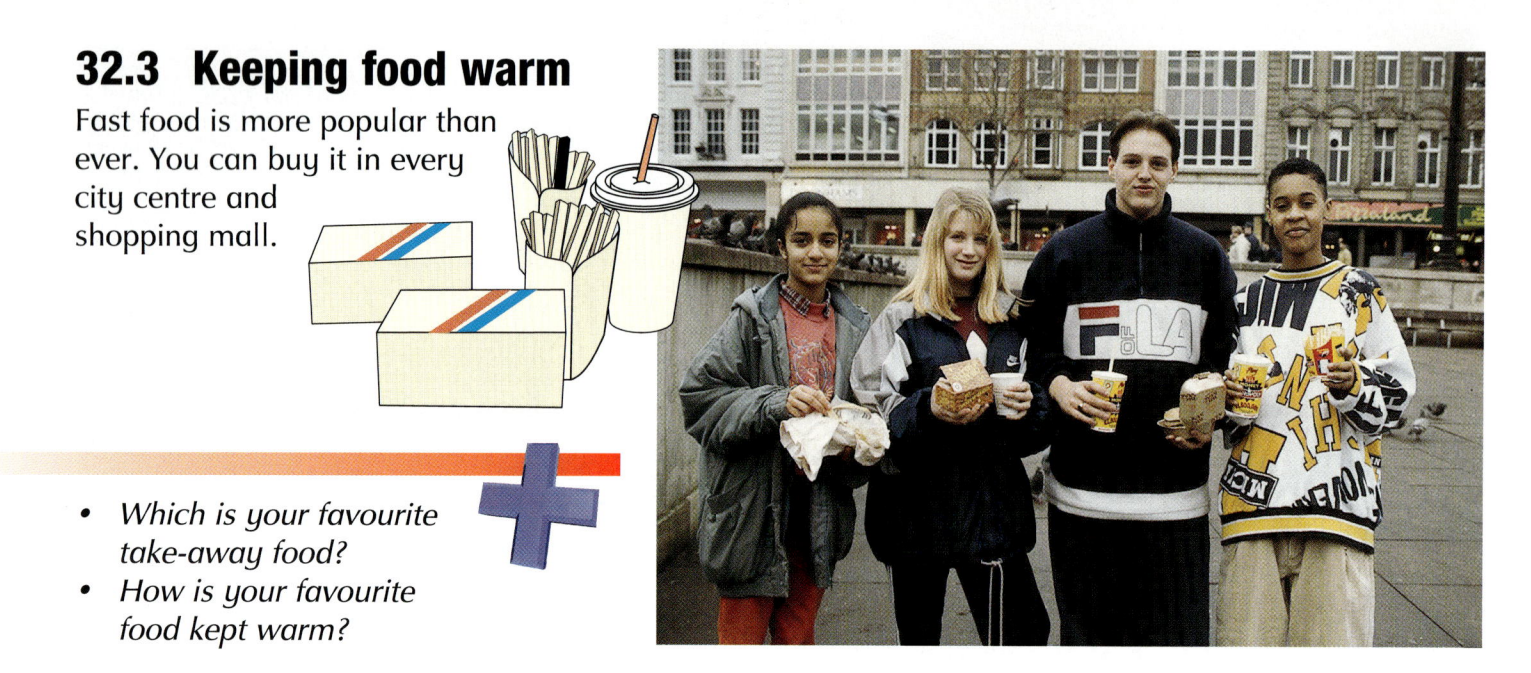

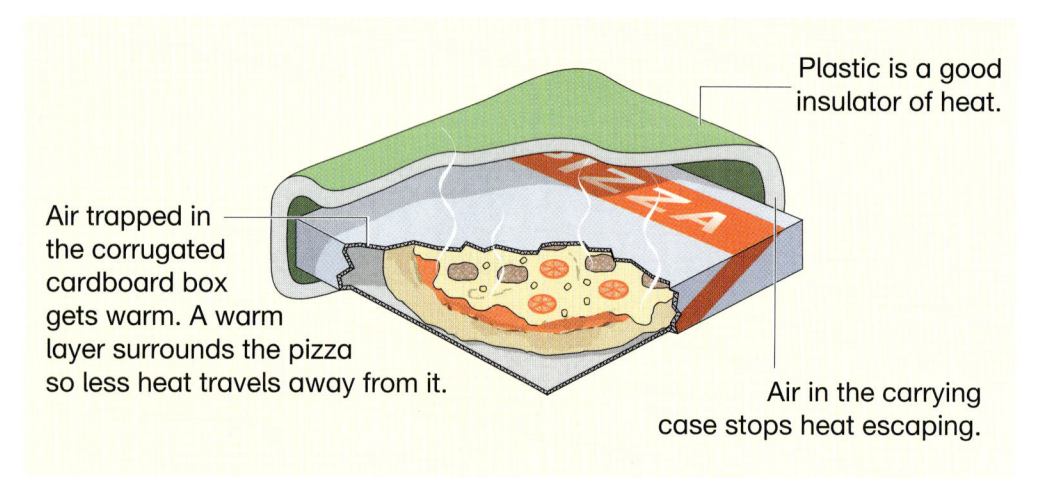

Air trapped in the corrugated cardboard box gets warm. A warm layer surrounds the pizza so less heat travels away from it.

Air in the carrying case stops heat escaping.

Most take-away food is hot so you need to keep it warm until you are ready to eat it. You have to stop the heat passing out through the packaging. Materials which slow down the movement of heat are called **insulators**. Plastic is a good insulator. Many insulators have small spaces which **trap hot air**. **Polystyrene** and **cardboard** have air spaces. Shiny materials reflect heat back. Metals **conduct** heat. Paper and card eventually **rot** away but plastic and polystyrene do not. Aluminium can be **recycled**.

1. List materials used to pack take-away food.
2. Which materials in the list are insulators?
3. How do pizza delivery firms keep pizza warm for their customers?
4. Design a range of containers for these take-away foods: baked potatoes, fish and chips, hot dogs.
5. Sort the materials in your list from Question 1 into a table with these headings: 'Can rot away', 'Cannot rot', 'Recyclable' and 'Non-recyclable'.

### Key words

**insulators**
**trapped air**
**polystyrene**
**cardboard**
**conduct**
**rot**
**recycle**

## 32.4 Using energy

- Where did he get the energy from to pull the aeroplane?
- How has your body used energy today?
- Where did you get your energy from today?

Energy exists in different forms. The main types of energy are **movement energy** and **stored energy**. Food has stored energy. Our bodies can transfer energy from food and use it to move. Energy is put into new chemicals to help us grow and repair our bodies. Energy not used straightaway is stored in fat around your body.

Heat is often given out when energy is transferred. So when we exercise we get hot.

- moving the body or other things
- keeping the heart beating
- repairing damaged parts of the body
- growing taller
- spare energy stored as fat

1. List all the energy transfers your body has made today. Show the changes as flow charts.
2. Which people in your class need a lot of energy foods? Why do they need extra energy?
3. Why do people who eat more energy food than they need get heavier?

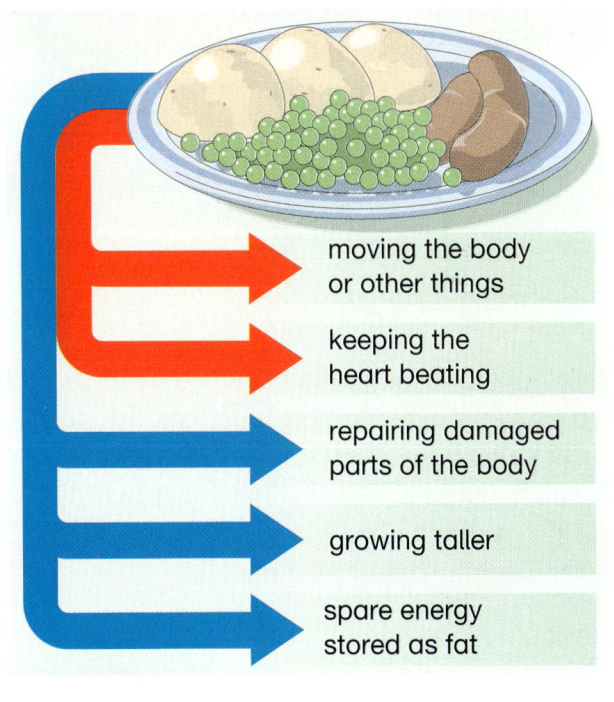

**Key words**

movement energy
stored energy

# 33 Movement

## 33.1 Pushes and pulls

We can push or pull on things to move them, stop them moving or change their shape. These pushes and pulls are **forces**.

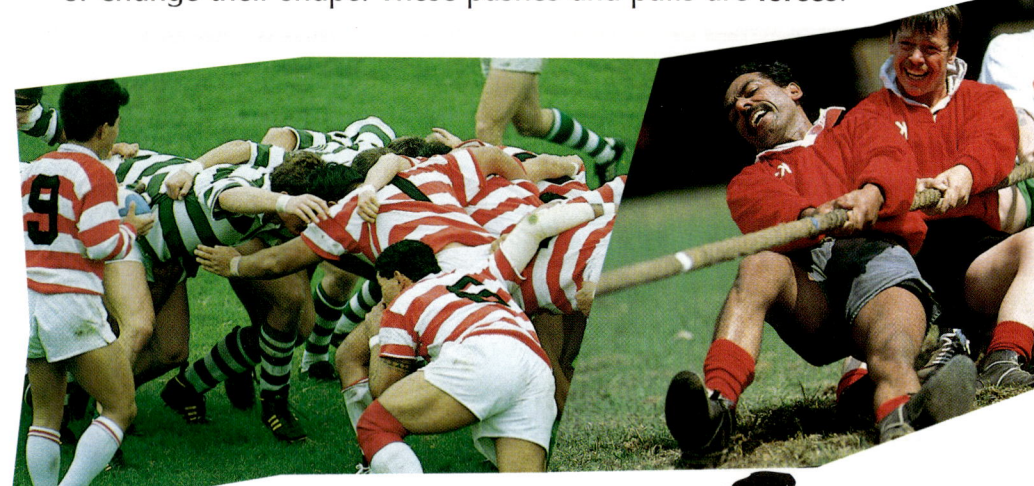

Wind blowing against the kite pushes it upwards.

Gravity pulls the kite down.

The string holds the kite in the best position to catch the wind.

- What is the best kind of place to fly kites?
- Is there a good place near where you live or near your school?
- Describe as many different kite designs as you can.

Kites have a large surface for the wind to **push** against. The person **balances** the **pull** of the wind by pulling on the string. Kites should be light so it is harder for **gravity** to pull them down. The kite stays in the same place if the forces are balanced.

1. List the forces you can see in the photographs on this page.
2. What happens when two equal forces pull against each other?
3. What would happen to a kite if the person let go of the string? Why?
4. What would happen to the kite if the wind dropped? Why?
5. What would happen if you pulled too hard on your kite?

**Key words**

force
push
balance
pull
gravity

## 33.2 Up, up and away

- Would you like to have a **hot air** balloon ride? Why?
- Describe hot air balloons you have seen.

A hot air balloon pilot makes the balloon go up by increasing the temperature of the air in the balloon. The **uplift** is bigger than **gravity**. The pilot makes the balloon go down by releasing hot air. The uplift is smaller than gravity. Pilots cannot steer the balloon. The wind pushes the balloon along. If there is not much wind the balloon stays still. All the forces are **balanced**.

1. Which force pulls a balloon towards the ground?
2. Name the force which makes a balloon rise.
3. What must a pilot do to make the hot air balloon go higher?
4. What would happen if the balloon got ripped? Why?
5. What makes the balloon travel from one place to another?
6. What would happen to the height of the balloon if the uplift and gravity forces were the same?

**Key words**

hot air
uplift
gravity
balance

## 33.3 Stopping forces

- Why do manufacturers drive new models of cars into walls?
- Why do we have a law which says you must wear a seatbelt in a car?
- Why is it dangerous to drive faster than the speed limit?

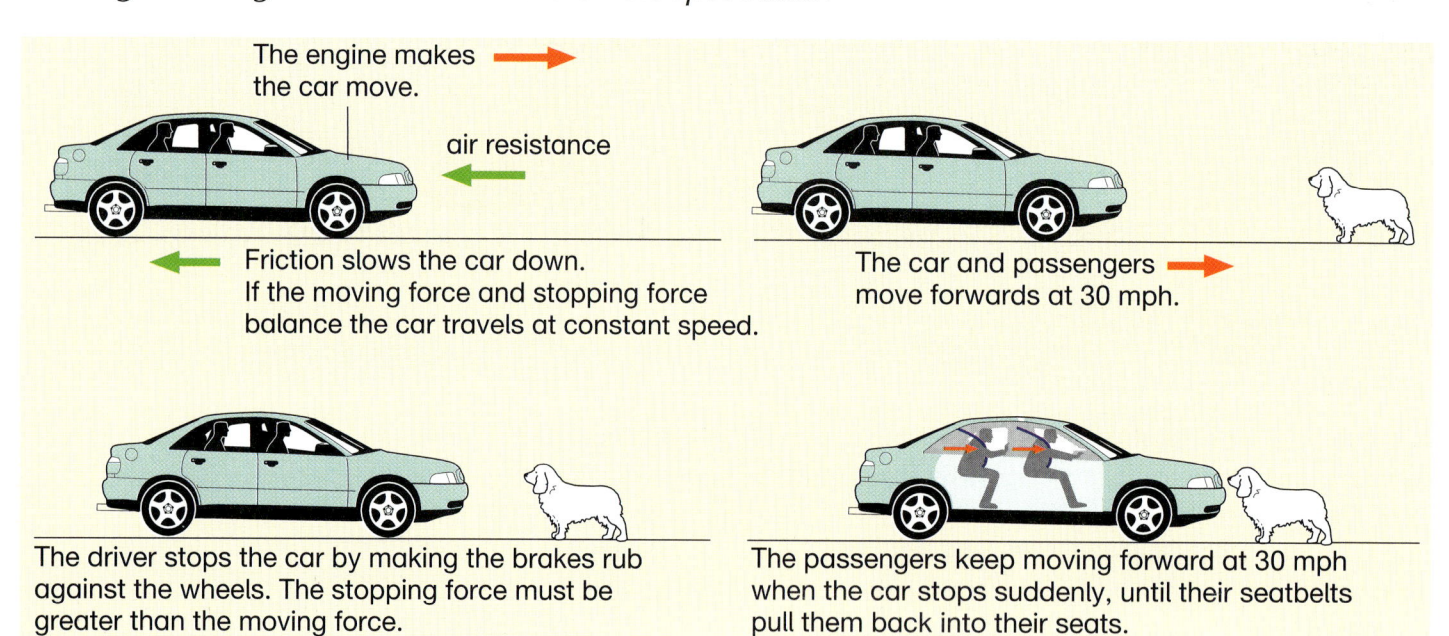

The engine makes the car move.

air resistance

Friction slows the car down. If the moving force and stopping force balance the car travels at constant speed.

The car and passengers move forwards at 30 mph.

The driver stops the car by making the brakes rub against the wheels. The stopping force must be greater than the moving force.

The passengers keep moving forward at 30 mph when the car stops suddenly, until their seatbelts pull them back into their seats.

**Friction** is a stopping force. **Rough** surfaces have more friction. **Brakes** work using friction. Fast **moving** objects need longer stopping distances.

1. What makes a car go?
2. List the things which make a car stop.
3. What is the name given to **stopping forces**?
4. What could happen if the brakes become worn away?
5. Why should car and bicycle owners replace worn tyres?

**Key words**

friction
rough
brakes
move
stopping forces

74

## 33.4 Keeping going

They used to be called bicycles – now they are **human powered vehicles** (HPVs)! Hundreds of Californians ride to work every day on these HPVs. There are no fuel bills, no pollution and plenty of healthy exercise. Are these the vehicles of the future?

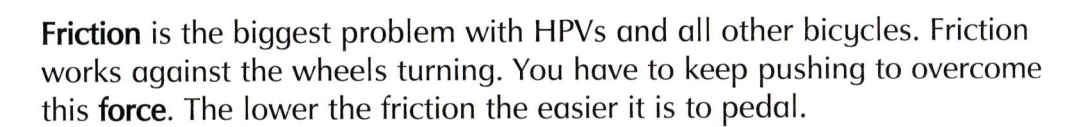

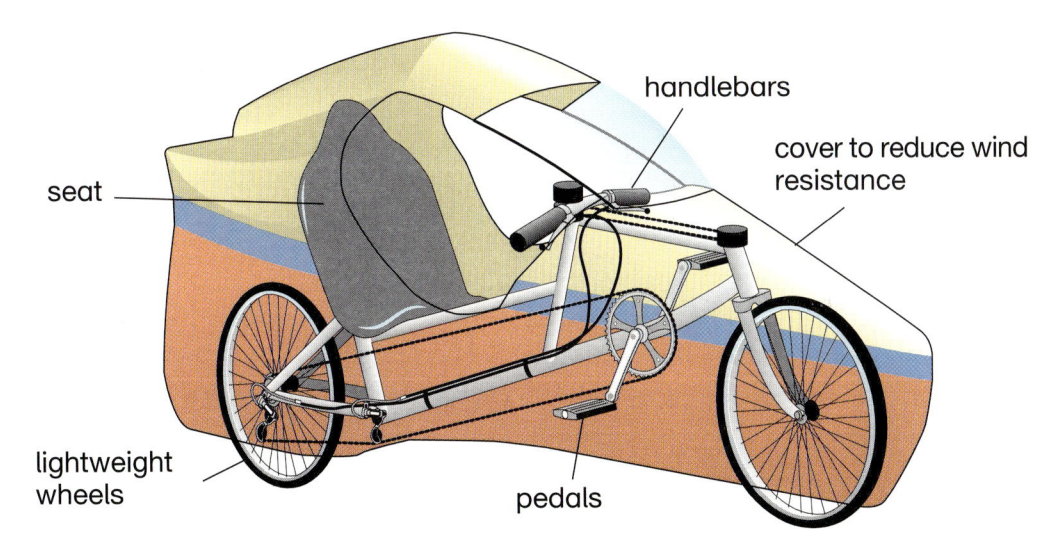

- How do you get to school in the morning?
- Would you be happy to travel by HPV? Why? Why not?

**Friction** is the biggest problem with HPVs and all other bicycles. Friction works against the wheels turning. You have to keep pushing to overcome this **force**. The lower the friction the easier it is to pedal.

*Labels on diagram:* seat, handlebars, cover to reduce wind resistance, lightweight wheels, pedals

1. List the features of the HPV. Explain how each one makes it easier to ride.
2. Design a buggy to travel as far as possible with only an elastic band to power it. Build and test your design.
3. Improve your design and then test it again.
4. When you have the best possible design draw it out and label it.

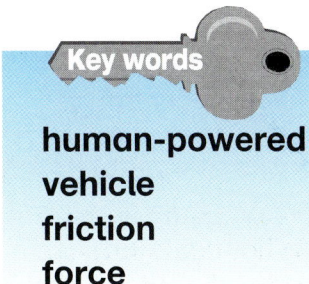

**Key words**

human-powered vehicle
friction
force

# Glossary

| | |
|---:|---|
| acid | a chemical which turns litmus paper red |
| addictive | habit-forming |
| agar | a jelly made from seaweed |
| air sac | a very small bag in the lungs that fills with air |
| airways | tubes that carry air when you breathe |
| alcohol | a compound found in beer, wine and spirits |
| algae | simple plants that live in water |
| alloy | a mixture of metals or metals and carbon |
| aluminium | a light silver-coloured metal |
| amalgam | an alloy of mercury |
| amplitude | the height of a soundwave |
| antibiotic | a substance that fights bacteria |
| arch | the part of a bridge between the pillars |
| ash | solid left after something has burned |
| asthma | a condition that narrows the airways |
| auditory nerve | carries impulses to the brain |
| bacteria | microscopic living things |
| balance | a simple weighing machine |
| beat | musical rhythm |
| biodegradable | broken down by bacteria |
| boiling point | the temperature at which something boils |
| bottle bank | collection point for waste glass |
| brakes | these grip wheels to slow or stop vehicles |
| bronchiole | a small tube in the lungs |
| bronchitis | when the bronchioles become infected and painful |
| bronchus | large tubes in the lungs |
| bud | the part of a plant which contains a new flower |
| carbon dioxide | a colourless gas that exists in very small amounts in air and is produced when a fuel burns |
| carbon | the most common element; contained by all living things |
| carnivore | animal-eating creature |
| catalyst | a substance which speeds up a reaction without being used up |
| cavity wall | a house wall with a hollow space down the middle |
| cement | a grey powder that is one of the ingredients of concrete |
| centre of gravity and centre of mass | the place in the middle of a solid object where its heaviness seems to be concentrated |
| centrifuge | spinning machine which separates mixtures |
| chemical changes or reaction | process whereby one chemical is changed into another |
| chromatography | a way to separate dissolved substances |
| chromoloy | an alloy of chromium |
| clay | fine-grained mud used to make bricks or pottery |

| | |
|---|---|
| combustion | burning |
| composite | a material made by combining two or more other materials |
| concrete | a mixture of cement, sand and gravel used in building |
| conduct | to let electricity or heat through |
| crockery | dishes |
| crude oil | unrefined oil |
| crystal | a pure piece of mineral with sharp edges and a regular shape |
| cycle | the way a substance returns back to where or how it started |
| data | facts from which other information can be gained |
| decant | to pour off the liquid, leaving behind the solid |
| decay | breaking down |
| decompose | to break down, rot |
| density | a measure of how heavy a substance is |
| desert | a very dry area of land |
| dialysis | the way waste substances are filtered from blood |
| diaphragm | sheet of muscle between the chest and the stomach |
| disperse | to spread around |
| distillation | a way of collecting a pure liquid from a mixture |
| dormant | alive but appears to be asleep; a dormant volcano is one that has not erupted for a long time |
| double glazing | two window panes with a small gap between them |
| draught excluder | used to stop warm air leaving from windows or doors |
| eardrum | thin vibrating layer between the outer and middle ear |
| echo | when soundwaves are reflected back so you hear it again |
| echo sounding | when ships send out soundwaves to measure the depth of the sea |
| efficient | not wasting energy |
| effort | the force you are using to move something |
| electricity | energy which flows down wires |
| enamel | a paint which produces a hard shiny surface |
| energy | the ability to make things happen |
| environment | the space around something |
| enzyme | a substance which changes the rate of chemical reactions |
| erupt | throw out lava, rocks and hot gas |
| eustachian tube | tube connecting the middle ear with the back of the mouth |
| evaporate | change from liquid to gas or vapour |
| extinguish | put out, such as a fire |
| extract | to take something out |
| ferment | when a substance turns into alcohol |
| filter | passing a mixture of a liquid and a solid through a sieve to separate them |
| flow chart | showing a sequence in pictures |
| flower | the part of a plant which reproduces the seeds |
| focus | seeing a sharp image |
| foil | thin sheet of metal |
| food chain | a diagram to show what animals eat |
| food web | a complicated food chain |
| force | a push or a pull |

| | |
|---|---|
| fossil fuel | fuel made from animals or plants which died millions of years ago |
| fractional distillation | separation of liquids by boiling points |
| frequency | the number of wavelengths in one second |
| friction | stopping force |
| fruit | the part of a plant which contains seeds |
| fuel | a material which gives out heat when it burns |
| fulcrum | the balance point of a lever; another word for pivot |
| fungi | plants that cannot make their own food |
| gas | the state of matter formed when a liquid boils |
| generator | makes electricity |
| germinate | starting to grow |
| glucose | a type of sugar |
| granite | a type of igneous rock |
| graphite | a form of carbon |
| gravity | a force which pulls objects together |
| grind | crush into a powder |
| heart disease | when the heart cannot work properly |
| herbivore | an animal that eats plants |
| human powered | made to work by human muscles |
| igneous | rock made when magma or lava cools |
| illusion | something that looks different from what it really is |
| inhaler | a container of chemicals which help you to breathe |
| insulate | to stop heat escaping |
| lactic acid bacteria | bacteria that make milk go sour |
| landfill site | a hole in the Earth where waste is dumped and then covered by soil |
| lava | hot liquid rock flowing on the surface of the Earth |
| lead | a heavy grey metal |
| leaf | part of a plant which makes food |
| lever | a simple machine, like a see-saw, with a fulcrum in the middle |
| limestone | a sedimentary rock made under water from the remains of tiny animals |
| load | the thing you are trying to lift or move with a machine |
| loam | garden soil containing a good mixture of sand, clay and dead plant material |
| machine | something that helps you do a job more easily |
| magma | hot liquid underground rock |
| mass | the amount of 'stuff' in something |
| mercury | a liquid silvery metal |
| metalised | plastic made to look shiny like metal |
| metamorphic | a type of rock made by heating and squashing other rocks |
| methane | a gas made when plants or animals rot |
| microscopic | so small that it can only be seen with a microscope |
| microwave | an oven which cooks food very quickly with radiation waves |
| mineral | a chemical that forms part of a rock |
| mixture | substance formed when ingredients are combined |
| mould | very small fungi |

| | |
|---|---|
| mudstone | a sedimentary rock made from small grains of mud pressed together |
| nervous impulse | signals that pass along nerves |
| nicotine | an addictive chemical found in tobacco |
| noise pollution | offensively loud |
| non-biodegradable | not rotted by bacteria |
| non-renewable | cannot be replaced |
| oil | thick greasy liquid made from plants and animals for fuel or food |
| oxygen | a colourless gas needed for burning and breathing |
| packaging | materials used to protect something |
| penicillin | a drug that kills bacteria |
| photosynthesis | how green plants use light to produce glucose |
| pillars | the vertical 'legs' of a bridge |
| pitch | how high or low a musical note is |
| pivot | the balance point of a lever; another word for fulcrum |
| plastic | an artificial material often made from oil |
| pollution | when waste materials spoil the environment |
| polystyrene | a kind of plastic |
| pressure | force produced by pressing |
| producer | a living thing used as food by other living things |
| protect | to keep something from harm |
| protein | chemical needed by the body for growth and repair |
| pull | a force which brings things together |
| push | a force which moves things apart |
| react | take part in a chemical change |
| reaction | a chemical change |
| recycle | to use again |
| reflect | send back again |
| renewable | able to be replaced |
| renewable fuel | fuel which can be replaced |
| resin | a kind of plastic |
| respiration | a chemical reaction which releases energy from food |
| restore | put back again, repair |
| rind | waxy covering |
| root | underground part of a plant |
| rot | break down |
| rough | bumpy |
| rust | chemical reaction between iron, water and air which leaves a reddish-brown coating |
| sandstone | a sedimentary rock made from grains of sand pressed together |
| seaweed | large algae that live in the sea |
| sedimentary | a rock made from grains of stuff pressed together |
| seed | contains a new plant |
| sell-by | the date after which goods are too old to be sold |
| sensation | feeling |
| sensor | the part that can detect a change |
| sensory nerve | a nerve which carries impulses to the brain |

| | |
|---|---|
| shoot | the part of the plant that grows above the ground |
| silica powder | a fine form of silicon oxide |
| smoke | fine powdered solids in the air |
| soggy | soaked with moisture |
| soil | material in which plants grow |
| solar power | energy from the sun |
| solder | an alloy of tin and lead with a low melting point |
| soluble | will dissolve |
| solution | a liquid with a substance dissolved in it |
| solvent | a liquid which can dissolve a substance |
| sound | what you hear |
| sour | sharp acid taste |
| source | place where a thing comes from |
| speeds up | gets faster |
| stable | hard to knock over |
| stem | supports leaves and flowers on a plant |
| stereoscopic | seeing two slightly different images as a 3-D one |
| stimulate | encourage something to begin |
| stopping force | a force which stops an object moving |
| stored energy | energy not being used at the moment |
| sugar | food made by plants or food that contains energy |
| survey | a way to find out what people think, often done by asking questions |
| survival | to continue to live despite danger |
| swamp | a waterlogged area in a hot country |
| symptom | sign that something is wrong |
| table | a set of facts arranged in columns |
| tar | thick black liquid |
| taste buds | small organs on the tongue that can taste substances |
| temperature | a measure of how hot something is |
| tin | a metal with a low melting point |
| tobacco | a plant used to make cigarettes |
| uplift | upward force in air or water |
| uranium | nuclear fuel |
| vegetable | roots and leaves which can be eaten |
| vehicle | a machine used for travel |
| vibration | moving back and forth in tiny amounts very quickly |
| volume | loudness |
| waterlog | soil with too much water in |
| wave | something that rises and falls as it moves; the form in which sound travels |
| wavelength | the distance from the start to the end of a wave |
| weight | how heavy something is |
| weld | to attach two metals by melting where they join |
| yeast | microscopic plant that causes fermentation |
| yoghurt | food made from milk |